the
UNHAPPINESS
SYNDROME

the UNHAPPINESS SYNDROME

28 HABITS OF UNHAPPY PEOPLE
(AND HOW TO CHANGE THEM)

Ryuho Okawa

IRH PRESS

BOOKS
IRH Press
New York

Library of Congress Cataloging-in-Publication Data

ISBN 13: 978-1-942125-16-7
ISBN 10: 1-942125-16-X

Printed in China

First edition

Book Design: Karla Baker

Cover/Interior Image © Fotolia / jessicahyde

PART III

THE UNHAPPINESS SYNDROME FOR WOMEN AND FAMILIES

6 Habits and Prescriptions for
Solving Marital and Home Problems

PART IV

THE UNHAPPINESS SYNDROME AT WORK

7 Habits and Prescriptions for
Surviving the Business World

PART V

THE UNHAPPINESS SYNDROME IN SPIRITUAL LIFE

*4 Habits and Prescriptions for
Overcoming Doubt and Fear*

preface

Multitudes of people in this world are unaware that they are suffering from their own love of unhappiness. The influence of one impetus or another pulls them headlong into their personal patterns of self-defeat because of this subconscious attraction to unhappiness. They are suffering from a condition that I call the *unhappiness syndrome*.

To end your relationship with unhappiness, above all other things you do, you will need to find the specific patterns that are defeating you. Only then will you open your path to freedom.

It is for this reason that I have written this book as a guidebook that walks you through the wide range of self-destructive patterns and offers my prescriptions for each of them. All accomplishments begin with knowledge, and I sincerely pray that the knowledge in this book will be the beginning of many happier lives throughout the world.

Ryuho Okawa
Founder and CEO
Happy Science Group

PART I

Are You In Love with Unhappiness?

Your Love of Unhappiness Could Be Interfering with Your Happiness

What do we desire more than anything else? The answer is happiness, of course—or so we all believe. In many years of dedicating myself to understanding and solving human problems, I have come across a curious truth about the human mind. Happiness is a basic human desire, we all would agree. But, oddly, I have found that many people are choosing thoughts and actions that create *un*happiness in their lives. To add to the confusion, I found that this pattern affects as many as 80 to 90 percent of people today.

Probably no one in this world would admit that they want to be unhappy. So how do we explain why so many people end up sabotaging their happiness? I have found that the cause lies in our mindset. What I discovered was a subconscious devotion to unhappiness. People are suffering from what I call the *unhappiness syndrome*, a condition in which the subconscious mind fosters a desire for unhappiness that manifests self-destructive thoughts and behavior. Put simply, many people are suffering from their own love of unhappiness. Within their minds are temples to the goddess of misfortune, not the goddess of success, and monuments to the god of poverty, not the god of prosperity.

> Many people are suffering from their own love of unhappiness.

How is it possible to repeatedly choose the opposite of what we consciously desire? After a lot

of contemplation, I have come to realize that, in most cases, people are simply unaware of their attraction to unhappiness. They are unable to stand back and see their thoughts and behavior as clearly as a detached observer would. As a result, they are unable to foresee where their thoughts and actions will ultimately lead them. They have good intentions, at least consciously. At a conscious level, they want to love and take care of themselves. But an external observer such as myself can nevertheless recognize an underlying devotion to self-hurt, self-blame, and self-persecution. Without a conscious awareness of the self-defeating patterns that control our thoughts, we can neither recognize them when they arise nor take the proper precautions to avert them.

I have assembled in these pages a collection of cases that I have diagnosed as manifestations of the unhappiness syndrome. These cases range from those that are typical of all of us, to those that commonly arise at work and home settings, to those that we find in our spiritual lives. If you read through the chapter titles and headings, you will no doubt recognize the ways that you, too, have fallen in love with unhappiness.

I wrote this book to help readers free themselves from self-sabotaging mental patterns and take charge of their own destinies. The prescriptions I offer are not just distilled from my personal musings but are also drawn from my examination of various scenarios I have come across over the course of years. And because these images of suffering remained so crisply in my heart, I decided to write as I would speak to each individual and as a close friend. The result, as you will see in the following chapters, is a simple, insightful outline of my secrets to life and happiness.

Recognizing the Unhappiness Syndrome Within You

We human beings have been granted full control over one important thing: our mind. We have no control over other people's thoughts. But our mind is the one realm where we stand wholly sovereign.

The secret to mastering life, therefore, is mastering one's mind. But the prevalence of negative thinking in the world is a telling indication that people are struggling to make use of this gift and, as a result, are suffering from the effects of a dismal outlook on life. We can find these people all around us—sitting in coffee shops, walking down sidewalks, browsing boutiques, working at their desks, waiting for the bus, and riding the train. I wish I could go up to everyone, point out their negative mindset, and explain how

that mindset will lead to unhappy outcomes.

It perturbs me that people allow negative thinking to pervade their mind even though they hold the power to change it. This stems from the fact that their minds have become habituated to these thought patterns, which exert a constant magnetic attraction to additional pessimistic circumstances.

An example of one way people typically react to other people's remarks offers a good illustration of the effects of negative thinking. As I have explained, the negative thinker's mind has fallen into a pattern of pessimism that leads to unhappiness. This means that when he hears a remark about himself, even if no malice was intended, it can set off a

negative reaction of hurt. His own mind will decide to attach a negative connotation to the words and allow him to hold onto this response for many years.

This illustrates how the subconscious desire to be unhappy exerts a natural, gravitational pull toward misery and misfortune. Just as the natural force of gravity requires no additional force to pull a roller coaster downhill, the negative thinker's mind, when left on its own, will naturally pull the mind into a downward spiral of distress.

In the chapters that follow, I describe a variety of cases, organized into several defining categories, to illustrate how this tendency of the mind manifests in our day-to-day lives. If you find that one of these cases reflects your own thought patterns, the crucial first step to take to start your self-transformation is to understand how this thought pattern is leading you to unhappiness.

Let me illustrate with an example. Some people have a pattern of reacting to other people's successes with envy and resentment. When a colleague beats them to a promotion, for example, they attribute his success

to his use of flattery or other methods of pleasing superiors. When a friend's business begins to show signs of profitable growth, they may try to undervalue her capabilities as an entrepreneur and ascribe her success to a fluke or a lucky break. They regularly verbalize their envy and bitterness to those around them, and they tend to believe beyond a shadow of a doubt that success will come to them, too.

> When we think envious thoughts or verbalize resentment, we are destroying our own chances for success.

How does this pattern result in self-defeat? My diagnosis as a spiritual counselor is that envy and resentment are emotions that sabotage our chances for success if we allow them to remain in our mind. When we think envious thoughts or verbalize resentment, we are destroying our own chances for success. Each time we make a negative remark about someone else's ability or good fortune, we are denying our own inner desire to achieve our

dreams. Our ideals need affirmative, positive reinforcement instead of destructive thoughts if we are to actualize them.

To help you understand the negative impact of these emotions, consider how they could influence the people around you. By verbalizing envious and resentful remarks, you are giving others the impression of an envious and resentful personality. Most people don't want to share their good fortunes and successes with someone who will react to them that way, so as a natural result of your thoughts and remarks, people will start to avoid you and stop inviting you to their get-togethers.

Most people who find themselves in this situation cannot understand why they are being ostracized by so many people. They sometimes regard themselves as having likable traits—for example, intelligence, good looks, eloquence, and even an exceptional work ethic—so they can't understand why they're constantly being left out. The more they're ostracized, the further they spiral into negative thinking. From an external observer's point of view, however, the source of their problems is clearly their own

resentful and envious attitude.

We can take a look at another example to understand how a negative thought pattern leads to unhappiness. Some people with a pessimistic view of life often feel a need to validate their negative beliefs in some way. This is one reason many people go to psychics or fortune-tellers. A psychic reading that confirms their pessimistic thoughts with an unfortunate future gives them a false sense of security. They feel that this foreknowledge will help them prepare for or at least endure their misfortune. This is the reason they are willing to pay twenty to thirty dollars to hear that they can expect to suffer a serious illness next year, a divorce in five years, death within the next ten years, or a child who may fall victim to a car accident.

We all live under the influence of destiny to some degree. Our lives are probably following some general path that we cannot completely change. But the purpose of life is not to surrender ourselves to ominous predictions, but rather to decide how we will steer ourselves through whatever life brings. Accepting someone else's negative predictions is the same as denying the true purpose that we are here to serve. This is clearly another pattern of unhappiness. We human beings are capable of conquering fate and steering our lives in the direction of our own choosing by gaining mastery over our own minds.

> We human beings are capable of steering our lives in the direction of our own choosing by gaining mastery over our own minds.

As my final example in this section, I would like to bring up a very common issue: financial problems. Financial problems essentially boil down to the issue of accumulated debt, so the obvious solution is to keep a balance sheet as a precaution against unintentionally spending more than you earn. While this is the obvious solution, some people continue to squander large amounts of money they do not own on gambling expeditions or high-risk investments, only to lead themselves further into a downward spiral of self-destruction. It is as if they are constantly chasing something that wants to lure them off the edge of a cliff into freefall. This something is unhappiness, and what is luring them is their subconscious attraction to it.

I wrote this book to spread awareness of this silent condition that is bringing suffering to so many people. It is my hope that this book will empower many people to take the necessary steps to resolve their patterns of unhappiness and take charge of their own destinies.

Finding Your
Patterns of Unhappiness

What can you do to stop the pattern of unhappiness from taking control? First, begin by realizing that you are in fact suffering from the unhappiness syndrome. More often than not, people haven't yet noticed the dissociation between their sense of self and the actual condition of their mind. Sometimes, this discrepancy is the chief issue. Many people believe that their mind is perfectly healthy when they are actually suffering. The vital foundation for healing is a clear awareness of our inner impulse for unhappiness.

So, rather than bemoaning why you are in such miserable circumstances, the first step is to look beneath the surface, put yourself into perspective, and see yourself just as you are. By doing so, you will gain a sense of your specific patterns of unhappiness. You are bound to relate to more than just one or two of the twenty-eight cases that I cover in this book. And since the unhappiness syndrome is so widespread, you shouldn't feel surprised if you recognize four or five, or even as many as ten, in your own habits of mind.

> The first step is to look beneath the surface, put yourself into perspective, and see yourself just as you are.

When you have identified your specific patterns, you will want to set up a strategy to help you stop your suffering from growing further. To come up with a plan, however, you will need to be able to see yourself from a higher standpoint. To cultivate this perspective, look to someone who is more knowledgeable and experienced than you are. This person will serve as your role model as you decide how to rise above your negative emotions and patterns of unhappiness.

Gaining an elevated perspective essentially means gaining mastery over your mind and restoring its pure, original state. It means mastering the skill of controlling your mind. This requires understanding the workings of the mind, and there is no surer way to do that than to understand the thoughts that are possible. As you discover new thought patterns and delve deeply into them, you will discover more solutions and methods for overcoming unhappiness, and all these solutions will become your own wisdom. For this reason, I hope that you will make use of the twenty-eight cases that this book introduces, for they are your promise of an end of unhappiness.

Four Signs that You've Ended Your Relationship with Unhappiness

To put an end to your unhappiness, you not only want to end your negative thinking, but also become and stay happy. Just as an airplane starts with liftoff and eventually reaches a cruising altitude at thirty thousand miles above the earth, we want to lift off by no longer thinking negatively and eventually maintain a constant state of happiness.

An essential tool for reaching your "cruising altitude" is a study of your unhappy experiences. A careful examination of your past should help you discern the specific negative patterns you are most prone to and show you how each of them affects your life. This way, you'll be able to recognize these patterns when they arise and return to happiness more quickly. Your ability to control your mind will improve,

and you'll be able to maintain longer and longer states of happiness.

Is there a way to measure whether you have become free of negative thinking? Yes! Four clear signs will help you determine whether you have reached a consistent state of happiness. When you are capable of maintaining all four indicators, you can be certain that you have conquered negative thinking.

> Do you get up feeling
> ready to take on
> the new day and
> believing that
> life is wonderful?

The first sign is waking up every morning feeling excited about life. Freedom from negative thinking

depends a lot on your state of mind when you get up in the morning. Do you get up feeling ready to take on the new day and believing that life is wonderful? You should feel confident about your happiness if, as you rise from your sleep every day, you feel grateful to be alive, thankful for another precious day, and filled with exuberant anticipation of a great day ahead. The reality of most people's mornings, however, is the opposite. Most people wake up feeling reluctant to go to work, uneager to see their spouse, unenthusiastic about having to work with their difficult colleagues, and loathing having to go through another long day. If your mornings are not full of positive anticipation and feelings of gratitude, this is the first goal you should aim for in your pursuit of freedom from negative thinking.

The second sign is a sense of vitality filling every inch of your body and a constant, eager itch to work. There are probably many people who have spent many decades drifting through life in desultory spirits, no longer able to remember how it feels to be enthusiastic or to feel passionate about their work and always feeling apprehensive about the future.

Being in such a condition of idleness and fatigue on a day-to-day basis only keeps happiness away.

> Whether you are happy or not depends on the images you allow to unfold in your inner world.

Ultimately, happiness is determined by your mental landscape. Whether you are happy or not depends on the images you allow to unfold in your inner world. Therefore, your happiness depends very much on how well you maintain your physical and mental stamina throughout life.

The average person is usually fatigued and suffering from depleted energy due to some combination of workplace stress, sleep deprivation, and a lack of exercise. So to determine whether you are happy, examine whether you are still capable of generating vitality—not the surface-level appearance of vitality, but the kind that wells up from within your depths. If you find this difficult to do, you will need to begin restoring your vitality and enthusiasm.

The third sign is the ability to see the wonderful aspects of everyone around you. Noticing only the negative aspects indicates a very dismal view of life. You probably see yourself as surrounded by villains who may try to harm you. This kind of pessimistic view of life can only result in unhappiness. It is extremely difficult to attract happiness with such a dark image of this world.

On the other hand, the ability to see the positive side of other people indicates that you have the heart of a wonderful person and is a clear formula for happiness. If you have not yet reached this state, try to find something positive about at least one or two people every day, and express your heartfelt compliments when you notice an admirable thought or action. To free yourself from negative thinking, make it your goal to notice and express the positive sides of those around you.

The final sign that you have conquered negative thinking is believing that you are here to serve a higher purpose beyond yourself. We gain a deep sense of happiness when we feel that we have contributed to other people's happiness or, to put it another way, when we realize that who we are has helped make this world a better place. Perhaps no other form of happiness can be greater than the joy we experience when the life we have chosen, the decisions we have made to follow our hearts, and the effort we put into being the best we can be all results in increased happiness for others.

> We gain a deep sense of happiness when we feel that we have contributed to other people's happiness.

I hope you will use these four signs of happiness as your guide as you go through each of the cases of the unhappiness syndrome described in the following chapters.

PART II

—

Common Symptoms of the Unhappiness Syndrome

11 HABITS AND PRESCRIPTIONS FOR CONQUERING SELF-DEFEATING THOUGHTS

1

"I Envy Other People's Successes"

The Person You Envy
Is a Reflection of Your Ideal Self

The first case of the unhappiness syndrome deals with the self-defeating tendency to envy the successful. If you are suffering from this negative thought pattern, you are probably already aware of the unhappiness inside you. If you follow my prescription, you can heal your mind of this negative pattern.

To begin the process of healing your mind, the first thing to do is to determine the cause of your feelings of envy. To do so, please look within your heart. You could literally place your hand over your heart if that helps you reflect inwardly. As your "soul physician," I would like to ask you to think back over your life and try to remember the times when

someone else's successes gave rise to emotions of envy within you. Can you distinguish the specific situations that were most apt to elicit these emotions? As you reflect, you should eventually notice a pattern: you didn't become envious when the success was outside your own areas of interest.

For example, if you work in the sales department of a major corporation, the chief focus of your energy and attention is enhancing your sales results. So, when one of your sales colleagues performs far better than you, your envy may become aroused. Let's consider the example of a salesperson at a car dealership. Put yourself into this salesperson's shoes.

You are able to sell two vehicles each month at best. But the star salesperson at your dealership, who is around the same age as you, has been selling fifteen vehicles a month. In this scenario, it's likely that you'll feel envious of his achievements. But why? It's because the job of selling cars is one of your own areas of interest.

On the other hand, you would not react the same way to the accomplishments of a professional baseball player, even if he hit ten home runs in a month. Perhaps you'd be disappointed if you happened to be a fan of a rival team, but you certainly wouldn't feel envious of him. This is because you are not a professional baseball player. Whereas, someone else who is a major league baseball player with a reputation for hitting home runs may feel envious of such an achievement.

We feel envious of people who achieve success in our areas of interest.

As we examine situations of envy in this way, we begin to gain a better understanding of

this emotion. We feel envious of people who achieve success in our areas of interest. What this means is that the person you envy is a reflection of your ideal. You wouldn't feel envious if you didn't have a desire to be like this person or to have what this person has achieved.

The people you envy are not your enemies or rivals, but your ideals. Deep down, you want to be like them or succeed as they have.

For example, if you envy your friend for having a charming and attractive boyfriend, these feelings indicate that you wish you could have an attractive boyfriend like hers, too. Because if her boyfriend had a horrible personality and weren't the type of guy you are typically attracted to, you most likely wouldn't envy her. It's because your ideal is to have a boyfriend with a similarly attractive personality and good looks that you cannot contain your feelings of jealousy and even have so much resentment that you end up drinking yourself into

a hangover or losing sleep over it. Your envy comes about because you want the same happiness and success that your friend has.

To conquer your feelings of envy, you will need to accept two facts. First, accept that your feelings of envy are indications that show where your interests lie. Second, understand that the people you envy are not your enemies or rivals, but your ideals. Deep down, you want to be like them or succeed as they have.

Consider Whether Your Ideal Is Realistic

My prescription for conquering envy begins with determining whether you have the potential to achieve your ideal. To do so, examine yourself from a detached point of view to gain a better understanding of your talents and abilities. Also, consider how others perceive your abilities. If your analysis shows that your chances of achieving your ideal are so slim that it would be as difficult as winning the lottery, that is a clear sign that this is not a realistic goal for you. For example, if your ideal is to become a royal princess, but your talents, abilities, appearance, and family background are very plain and average, it's very unlikely that you'll be chosen to marry into a royal family, even in this day and age. The princesses we see around the world possess certain conditions and attributes that make them well-qualified for the high-profile role of royalty. When you take this into account, you can easily determine whether you are really qualified to become a royal princess. And if you conclude that you have no chance of attaining this dream, then there's no purpose in envying the women who have been chosen as princesses.

If your ideal is so beyond your grasp, then let go and look for realistic ideals that reflect your true potential.

As this example shows, what we need to do with unrealistic ideals is simply let them go and cast them wholly out of the mind. Don't allow your envy to seep into your mind. Simply refrain from thinking about your feelings of envy; when those feelings come, let them flow past you and slip away. This is the best course of action. But you may wonder whether giving up is really the right thing to do. In this regard, my next piece of advice is to change your ideals. Your intention should not be simply to give up everything, but rather to adopt a different ideal that aligns with the ideal you were truly born to achieve. Of course, there may be cases in which the successes that you envy are within reach of your true potential. But if your ideal is so beyond your grasp that you don't stand a chance, then my prescription is to let go and look for realistic ideals that reflect your true potential.

Look to Those You Envy as Role Models of Success

But what should you do if you do have the potential to achieve your ideal? Let's consider a professional baseball player who is fifth in the batting order and whose ideal is to become third and then improve further to eventually become fourth. This is an ideal that definitely has potential and is likely to be achieved if the player puts the necessary effort into it.

In this situation, we should not let ourselves wallow in our envy, but instead accept that the person we envy is a reflection of our ideal. We should shift our mindset and look to this person not as an object of resentment but as a role model who can show us who we want to become. By shifting

our perspective this way, we will be more likely to recognize the exceptional attributes in this person that are lacking in ourselves. These attributes are the clues to success that we want to learn from and develop in ourselves.

It is vital to learn from the people we envy and to consider them our role models, because that will help us improve our own chances of success. It will require careful observation and analysis, but there is always something exceptional about these people that allows them to produce remarkable results. Let's return to the example of the car salesman. In his situation, we cannot

conclusively say that he has no chance of achieving his ideal; he may have the potential to become a star salesman. He can do so by carefully studying how the star salesman was able to achieve his success.

Behind any remarkable achievement, there are always certain reasons and conditions that made it possible. For example, he may have developed a wide network of connections. He may also be using a special technique to persuade customers to agree to his deal. Perhaps he also pays attention to his suit and overall appearance in particular ways. And there may be hints in the way he pitches his offer and the way he speaks to the customers when he calls them. Careful observation will likely reveal several clues to his success.

Making a study of his successes may not help you sell fifteen cars right away, but it will help you gradually improve your performance. From selling two cars a month, you may jump to three, then eventually six, and gradually you will move all the way up to fifteen. When you finally reach your goal of selling fifteen cars, that is the moment when your rivalry truly begins.

During this process of learning from your role model, you should remember to never put down or disparage his achievements. Instead, it is important for you to respect him as your role model and look to him as a valuable person to learn from. It is very important to cultivate a positive attitude toward him and his success.

> We must look to those who are successful as our role models from whom we can learn the keys to success.

In conclusion, we envy successful people because they have succeeded in an area of our own interest and represent the person we want to become. They are a reflection of our ideals. So to overcome our envy, we must begin by accepting them as a reflection of our ideals. Then we must determine whether these ideals are realistic for us, and if they are not, we must let go of them and replace them with different ones that reflect our true potential. From then on, we should put our all into them and

persevere until we succeed. But if we do have the potential to reach our original ideals by working hard, then we must not envy or disregard those who are successful, but instead look to them as our role models from whom we can learn the keys to success. Making these efforts will, without a doubt, transform your negative patterns of envy into positive ones that are productive, elevated, and noble.

2

"My Enthusiasm Is Completely Gone"

The Key Is to Generate Your Own Enthusiasm

Before I explain my solution, we should begin by considering why you are suffering from sagging enthusiasm in the first place. Why has your enthusiasm disappeared? It is essentially because you have allowed yourself to accept an apathetic attitude toward life. This apathy comes from holding a negative self-image within your mind.

An apathetic attitude is the feeling of drifting aimlessly, day after day, with very small ideals and no conscious sense of where you want to go in life. Put simply, you have no clear sense of direction or purpose. When you think about it, you may realize that you are going through the day just wishing for luck to come to you, like finding a four-leaf clover on the sidewalk. Or you may be going through the day thinking that maybe if you won the jackpot or the lottery, then your enthusiasm might come back to you.

Lack of enthusiasm can be caused by a wide range of things that vary from person to person, so I can't generalize one case to everyone who struggles with this problem. While one person's exhaustion may be caused by a physical condition, such as physical exhaustion or an illness, someone else may be struggling with a sense of failure from having made a big mistake at work. Still others are suffering from deep heartbreak after repeatedly falling in love only to have their heart broken. So I don't know what

specifically has caused your sagging enthusiasm, but I do have a prescription that will help restore your enthusiasm for life.

The first thing to do is to understand the reason for your loss of enthusiasm. When you examine the thoughts behind your desultory attitude, you should recognize a deep-seated belief that you will end up a failure no matter what you try to do. As you dive deeper into what has caused you to feel this way, you will probably realize that it's the result of a setback you went through at some point.

The next step is to decide what you want to do about your situation. Do you want to remain where you are? Or do you want to change? One thing is certain: simply waiting for your enthusiasm to return is unlikely to work. It's as unlikely as a gift from outer space falling into your lap or discovering Aladdin's lamp and being able to make a wish to reawaken your enthusiasm and succeed in your business.

Of course, an asteroid does very occasionally fall through the earth's atmosphere, so if you feel

that the best you can do right now is be still and wait for your enthusiasm to return or for something else to awaken your enthusiasm for you, then wait you will, no matter how long that it may take. There are also some cases in which dissipated enthusiasm is only a temporary phenomenon, and leaving it alone until it returns is one way of dealing with it.

> If your heart feels even a sliver of desire to improve your current condition, that's a sign of your potential for tremendous improvement.

But if you want, you can begin to change right now by taking the third step, which is picturing to yourself the best that you can be. If you are able to hold a clear mental picture of your ideal self, or if your heart feels even a sliver of desire to improve your current condition, that's a sign of your potential for tremendous improvement.

Set Small Goals to Motivate Yourself

Once you've taken these three steps and are ready to restore your enthusiasm, what do you do to bring it back? When you feel that your enthusiasm is completely gone, there is only one real way to bring it back, and that is to *make* yourself an enthusiastic person. Essentially, you create your own enthusiasm.

What I recommend as the best way to regenerate enthusiasm is setting reachable goals. This is the "carrot on a stick" method, and I have found it an effective way of motivating yourself and pulling yourself out of inertia. Right now, you are most in need of realistic, reachable goals, just as an exhausted horse needs a carrot to be motivated to push forward again.

To continue the carrot analogy, you should pay careful attention to the kind of carrot you choose and where you decide to put it. Set it as close to you as possible, at just the right height to ensure that it is within reach. It should also be small enough that you will be able to bite half of it off on the first try. In other words, set a realistic goal so that you can taste success quickly and gain

the motivation to keep working toward new goals.

The point I would like to emphasize is that for a goal to motivate you, it must be attainable; you will defeat the purpose if you set it one or two miles away from you. The goal needs to be placed right in front of you, just as the carrot on the stick is literally set inches from the horse's eyes.

> What you are in need of in your current state is to be able to savor a sense of accomplishment and remember the taste of success.

The second element I would like to emphasize is that this goal shouldn't be too grand or idealistic. Choosing a goal that is so ambitious that you're unlikely to reach it during your lifetime will not help you restore your sagging enthusiasm. Your enthusiasm needs a goal that is simple and within your grasp but that will give you a sense of accomplishment. What you are in need of in your

current state is to be able to savor a sense of accomplishment and remember the taste of success.

You want a goal that you can reach by taking simple steps and making small improvements to your life. So if you are a college student, acing all the courses that you are taking this semester is not the kind of goal you want to choose. Instead, set a narrower goal of improving your exam scores in one of the courses you're not doing as well in or improving your grades further in one of the courses you are doing well in. Resolve to improve in one course, and that's enough to begin with.

Next, consider a company worker whose job performance has been suffering and who's clearly struggling with sagging enthusiasm. My advice to him is the same: he should refrain from trying to accomplish too many things at the same time and instead should calmly consider what he can do immediately to make simple and attainable improvements to his work and performance.

For example, he might begin by organizing his desk and office. A very common cause of exasperation and frustration in the workplace is the state of chaos

that papers and files are often left in, which keeps impeding progress. Believe it or not, this is a very common reason why business-people can develop irritable and restless personalities. If your work space feels chaotic, the first thing to do is clean up your desk and organize your files. Sort your papers and files into separate piles for those that need attention and those that have been completed. Then, you can go through the pile that needs attention and set specific deadlines and file away the pile that has been completed. Just by taking these simple steps to organize your work area, you will be able to restore vital clarity and begin to feel motivated again.

The same basic principle applies to situations at home. Even when you know that you need to clean your messy house, there are times when you cannot seem to get yourself to do it. One reason for your lack of motivation may be that your house is too large for you to keep up with. Another reason could be that as soon as you finish cleaning, your family makes a mess again, and this leaves you frustrated.

One simple step you can consider to improve this situation is asking your spouse to put his or

her belongings away where they belong. If your spouse agrees, that will help prevent messes. If the problem is your children, not your spouse, there are ways you can educate your children to clean up after themselves.

Sometimes the problem may be completely due to your own lack of motivation. There are simple steps you can take in this case, too. For example, you can assign different cleaning tasks to different days of the week to make your goals more attainable and less overwhelming. Perhaps you can designate one room to each day of the week; Monday could be the day you tackle the bathroom, Tuesday the kitchen, Wednesday the living room, Thursday the bedroom, Friday the backyard and flower garden, and so on. Your motivation may be

sagging because you feel overwhelmed by the idea of cleaning your entire home at once, and then you end up waiting for spring cleaning to get to it.

If even these simple steps don't help you feel motivated and you'd rather wait for enthusiasm to come to you or be given to you from somewhere else, then I have no solutions to offer. There is nothing I can tell you except that you'll just have to wait for it to come.

But if you want to do something to improve your situation, and you are willing to take the necessary action, then my best advice is to begin with something attainable and realistically achievable. Aim to make simple, basic improvements to your situation. If you do so, I am certain that your enthusiasm will return.

3

"I Live in Constant Fear of Being Hurt"

Fear of Getting Hurt Is a Result of Past Bitter Experience

Living in constant fear of being hurt can be a struggle in itself. The feeling of fear alone may be enough to dissolve all hopes of happiness. Perhaps no one who suffers from this fear would profess to ever feeling happy. In this sense, fear of being hurt may well be the self-defeating thought pattern that best exemplifies how the unhappiness syndrome manifests in our day-to-day lives.

It's important to begin with an understanding that this is a quintessential dilemma of the human species. This particular fear arises from our natural urge to live in large communities. Because we are social by nature, our happiness or unhappiness is never wholly immune to influence from those around us and the rest of human society. Just as our own behavior can bring someone joy or sadness, other people's behavior can affect our state of mind. This is an aspect of life that we need to accept.

If you are surrounded by good-natured men and women who offer benevolent support, bring positive news, and help you succeed, then it won't require much effort at all to feel content and happy around them. On the other hand, if you are surrounded by people who frequently disparage, criticize, and distrust others, then happiness may feel like a scarce luxury. If the latter case applies to you, you probably see the world as abundant with hostile and harmful things.

When we closely examine those who have developed this view of the world, we will most likely find many people who are carrying the emotional baggage of some hurtful experience of the past.

> Just as our own behavior can bring someone joy or sadness, other people's behavior can affect our state of mind.

Just as the fear of dogs is triggered by the terrible memory of having been barked at or bitten at one time or another, probably during childhood, the fear of being hurt by another person is most often triggered by the trauma of a painful experience in the past. For a child, the frightful bark or bite of an angry dog can be so traumatic and impactful that the sight of a dog even in adulthood might elicit fear. Likewise, if you have ever felt hurt or betrayed, the pain could be imprinted in your memory and create the fear of becoming victim to a similar experience again.

For example, those who have gone through the pain of breakups with multiple partners are more likely to develop a deep-seated belief that any man or woman is eventually going to leave them. This belief turns into fretting, and fretting turns into a hunt for "signs" to validate the suspicion that a new partner is going to bring heartache once again.

The workplace is another place where people struggle with the effects of past trauma. It's common for two colleagues going out for drinks together to have a relaxed and open conversation, especially if they consider one another to be trustworthy and show genuine concern for each other's well-being. As friends are meant to do, it's common for one colleague to trust and confide in the other about, for example, a mistake that she is struggling to bring up with her superior. But what happens if she discovers the next day that her superior has found out about it and wants to know what is going on? She confided in her colleague and spilled all the details because she thought she could trust him, and she even thanked him for being a true friend, but now she feels betrayed.

Situations like this are commonplace, especially in the competitive world of business. Some people

believe it is their job to behave like police dogs and be on the hunt for suspicious activity to report to their superiors. They try to appeal to their superiors with their sense of loyalty. Some may even deliberately pretend to be your friend only to turn their backs on you. Meanwhile, their superiors find them quite useful because they help safeguard against potential problems.

The people who are betrayed, however, tend to feel the effects of the pain for some time, and some of them may even vow never to confide in anyone again. But this only isolates them from their coworkers.

Other commonplace scenarios include rumors about private matters that are spread to hurt people's reputations and stall their prospects of promotion. There are a multitude of scenarios like these, and when they happen they hurt people. That pain can develop into a constant fear, an inability to trust others, and a hard, isolated shell into which the victim withdraws.

A Positive Self-Image Will Create an Aura that Will Shield You from Hurt

When we carefully examine people who believe that they are constant victims of hurt, what do you think we will find? Interestingly, we will discover that the fault does not belong only with those who impose the hurt. Close study will show a common element among victims, and that is an aura of the victim complex. That is to say, they give others the impression that they always feel hurt and are anticipating that more painful situations will befall them.

For example, a typical mistake that they make is carelessly exposing their weaknesses, offering others an opportunity to rub salt in their wound. This is a result of a deficiency of proper self-love. They have a subconscious desire for self-destruction that accidentally manifests again and again. A past setback or failure most likely brought about a strong sense of self-depreciation that took root deep inside them and continues to tell them that they are unworthy,

are nothing, and won't amount to anything.

> Picture in your mind how God imbued your life with His own breath and with a duty to achieve happiness.

If you find yourself in these circumstances, my prescription is to use positive thinking to pull yourself through the effects of your subconscious thoughts. If you continue to allow yourself to believe that you are a nobody or that you are not good enough to achieve greatness, you will only be left with a hopeless sense of despondency. These negative thoughts need to be turned around and replaced by a strong belief that you are a child of God and a superb human being. Draw a strong image in your mind, as you live from day to day, of your God-given right to be happy. Picture in your mind how God imbued your

life with His own breath and with a duty to achieve happiness.

By doing so, you will eventually exude such positivity that no one will be able to criticize you for fear that it will only come back to them. No one will be able to hurt you anymore, because when you are constantly emanating joyfulness, cheeriness, and an air of success, anything negative that anyone says about you ends up reflecting badly on them and giving others the impression that they may be the ones being resentful about you.

In displaying a dejected attitude or a despondent atmosphere, you are practically handing others reasons to agree with any negative remarks that others spread about you. By examining your dilemma from this perspective, you will see how essential it is to stop finding fault in others and begin taking the responsibility to conquer this problem by cultivating healthier self-esteem, changing your attitude, and changing your atmosphere.

Take Simple Measures to Exude Positive Energy

What can you do to create a positive atmosphere and cultivate a positive self-image? In essence, you give others the sense that terrific things are happening to you, which you do by taking delight in life's simple pleasures and discovering the seeds of happiness and success within your surroundings. Even when you are feeling down from the troubles you need to deal with, you can use simple techniques to change your mood. You can freshen up your outfit with a brand-new, high-quality tie in a style you normally wouldn't choose. Perhaps you could choose a cheerful color, like red. You could also treat yourself to an evening of fine dining at an acclaimed restaurant, order a tailor-made suit or dress, or buy yourself the pretty heels you've been eyeing for so long. Giving a new twist to your day-to-day routine is a very simple way of lifting your spirits.

If your marital relationship has been suffering through a phase of heavy bickering, making a simple change in your appearance can make a surprisingly big difference.

Your spouse may just be frustrated to see you in the same recycled outfits every day. By trying on something different and elegant, you'll pique your spouse's curiosity and spark an enjoyable conversation. When your spouse asks if something special has happened to you, you could just say, "Nothing in particular," to further interest his or her curiosity for an even better chance of an enjoyable time together.

> Hurtful situations are ultimately the result of your own attitude.

There is any number of steps like these that will add a new flavor to your day-to-day routine and bring a sense of cheer back into your life. It's the simple efforts we make in our day-to-day lives that open up new avenues of hope for our future. Simple measures like these can end hurtful situations by creating an air of success and happiness.

Hurtful situations are ultimately

the result of your own attitude; the cause does not lie in others. When your feelings are hurt by someone's unkind remarks, you may be exaggerating their importance. Some people never allow themselves to be fazed by negative remarks. They simply let the words slide past them as if nothing had happened. It is their strong sense of self-confidence that allows them to do this.

But if you have low self-esteem, you might be inclined to believe others' negative remarks, in which case of course their words will sting. This is another reason why I continue to stress how invaluable it is to build a positive and constructive self-image.

After you have made all these changes to your day-to-day attitude and successfully brought cheer back into your life, the next step to creating an aura of positivity is to take proactive actions, such as complimenting other people.

What happens to you while you are facing a crisis or in the midst of despair? You probably find it difficult to focus on anything except the miserable circumstances that are overwhelming you. That tight focus makes you oblivious to the lives of the people around you. Even when you receive a compliment, you may be so absorbed in your image of self-defeat that it only sounds like flattery to you. Your mind can become completely attached to your self-image of despair.

> While the future closes the doors to those who lay blame on others, it will open avenues of hope to those who make the resolute decision to change themselves.

I believe that no other situation in life calls more strongly for giving compliments than when we are lost in despair. Rather than mulling over dire circumstances, shift your attention to those around you. Try to find something nice about them, and then tell them. If they are great people, let them know that. And if you enjoyed your meal, say so out loud, and tell others how much you enjoyed it.

By being proactive and taking concrete steps to express a positive attitude, such as by giving people compliments, we open new avenues to the future. When we suffer from this symptom of the unhappiness syndrome, we need to remember that the key is not expecting others to change, but persevering to change our own attitude from negative to positive.

The same prescription applies to those who struggle with a low self-esteem due to poor academic performance or a lower level of intelligence. We might think it's right to attribute people's criticism to our academic background or our level of intelligence, but we should be encouraged to remember that there are a multitude of poorly educated people who are nevertheless accomplished and successful. Our hurt feelings are the result not of our background, but of our low self-esteem. Our low sense of self-worth is causing us to feel pain and making us believe that people are trying to harm us.

The solution, therefore, is to persevere until you are able to produce results that show your true capabilities. Keep working to let people see how outstanding you are; your hard work will stop people from criticizing you.

While the future closes the doors to those who lay blame on others, it will open avenues of hope to those who take complete responsibility for their problems and make the resolute decision to change themselves.

4

"I Struggle with Asserting Myself"

Self-Assertiveness Is about Expressing Our God-Given Individuality

Many people quite understandably struggle to determine how best to assert themselves. This dilemma has a lot to do with self-assertion's dualistic nature: it can work either positively or negatively, depending on how it is used. This is the reason why we have a hard time telling whether our self-assertiveness is positive or negative. Many examples throughout human history prove that self-assertiveness has played an essential role in the achievements of men and women of greatness, and this fact makes it trickier.

Let's examine self-assertiveness to gain a better understanding of it. The essential question we want to consider is why we humans naturally feel a desire to assert ourselves and be noticed. Where does this desire come from? Does it arise from an evil side of our ego? There are two basic reasons why we all have some degree of self-assertiveness.

> God endowed us with the gifts of individuality and self-expression so we can express our differences.

First, self-assertiveness arises from a desire to express our individuality. A fragment of God lies within each of us, and all of us are equal as children of God. At

the same time, however, God also gave us the freedom to develop into unique individuals. Having unique personalities means that the differences between people become emphasized, and this was God's intention. He endowed us with the gifts of individuality and self-expression so we can express our differences. This is the root of our desire to assert our unique qualities.

In this sense, self-assertiveness is neither evil nor wrong. We can compare each person's endeavor to express his or her uniqueness with a flower's effort to grow a little taller and a little more beautiful than the rest. In this sense, all things in nature assert themselves too. No one would condemn flowers for trying to express their individual beauty, and it is just as absurd to say that self-assertiveness is an expression of evil.

Second, self-assertiveness arises from a desire to enhance our worth as individuals. We all want to be capable of greatness, be valuable, and be recognized. These desires are an inherent,

valuable part of being human. Without these desires, we wouldn't be able to feel the aspiration to serve society and contribute to the advancement of civilization. Our sense of self-respect and desire to achieve greatness has been the vital, driving force that has encouraged humankind to contribute to the development and evolution of our societies.

Ultimately, self-assertiveness represents the human soul's strong wish to feel valuable to those around us and, therefore, to be recognized for our accomplishments. Within the depths of the human soul lies a strong hope or energy that seeks continual progress.

In conclusion, self-assertiveness arises from the desire found within each person's soul to be a unique individual, become a better version of ourself, earn respect, and evolve further to greatness. Ultimately, we find nothing inherently wrong with self-assertion itself. The dilemma we face is determining how strongly we should assert ourselves.

With Positive Self-Assertion, You Won't Impinge on Others' Happiness

If self-assertiveness is an inherent aspect of the human soul, does that mean that there is no use in trying to curb it and there is nothing we can or should do about it? We know that we cannot completely eliminate our desire to assert ourselves, because self-assertion is an inherent and purposeful part of human individuality and achievement. That said, a dilemma arises when we consider self-assertiveness in relation to the people around us. The question we need to ask is not only how to grow and accomplish great things as individuals, but also the effects that our self-assertion will have on other people's happiness.

Let's return to the example of the flower. We might say that the beauty of a garden is made possible by the hard work and effort that each flower puts into competing with the other flowers and becoming as beautiful as it possibly can. As a result, flowers are capable of transforming plain landscapes into scenes of exquisite beauty. This achievement is the flowers' source of pride and happiness.

On the other hand, consider what would happen if one particular kind of flower begins to dominate a landscape. Even if it's the most beautiful flower known to humankind, it's still impinging on the happiness of the other plants and flowers that have made this place their home and are flourishing blissfully. This would certainly result in tragedy.

This phenomenon occurs in reality in natural habitats. When one species of a tree or fern proliferates too rapidly, it may reduce the available sunlight and consume vital nutrients that other plants in the area need, making it impossible for them to survive.

> The essential factor to consider is whether your self-assertion will harm others and encroach on their happiness.

This is the reason that self-assertiveness can become a problem. When we are able to foster a healthy coexistence with others, self-assertiveness can play a positive role. However, when self-assertiveness results in the dominance of one group over the welfare of others, this gives rise to unhappiness.

Should some degree of self-assertiveness be allowed, even when it interferes with other people's happiness? Let's return to the example of the flower one more time. Most people probably wouldn't be disconcerted to find their garden overtaken by beautiful flowers; in fact, it might bring them joy. But if these were weeds, rather than colorful blossoms, it would be an altogether different story. No one would want to find weeds monopolizing their beautiful garden and lawn—that's why we invest the time and money to maintain them throughout the seasons.

As this example illustrates, the essential factor to consider is whether your self-assertion will harm others and encroach on their happiness. This is an important way to help you keep your assertiveness in check.

If you are young and struggling with a tendency to be very assertive, which is understandable especially in youth, then you probably have a lot of capability and vitality. You should keep persevering on the path you are on. And my advice to you is this: always pay attention to how you affect those around you so as not to cause others harm. This is the essential point we need to reflect on to help us determine how best to assert ourselves. Being able to put your all into your work may bring you a sense of self-gratification, but it is important to reconsider the way you are approaching your work if it is making others feel unpleasant or unhappy.

Building Solid Self-Esteem Curbs Aggressive Self-Assertiveness

If you are struggling with strong self-assertiveness, my advice is to try to put your abilities to use in a much gentler fashion. Try to bring more balance to your approach to life. Those who are aggressively self-assertive have become this way because they are in a big hurry to gain recognition and are too focused on producing

immediate results. In other words, they are seeking other people's approval.

This tendency to focus on other people's approval is an indication that you don't yet conclusively approve of yourself. You are probably feeling unsure of yourself and so keep seeking other people's validation. Your sense of self-esteem and confidence becomes very shaky without constant approval.

> To develop that confidence, you must stop seeking approval from others and instead seek approval from yourself.

What you must do first is develop a strong foundation of positive self-esteem. That is to say, you need to feel confident about your self-worth. To develop that confidence, you must stop seeking approval from others and instead seek approval from yourself. Examine your self-perception on a daily basis, and make sure that whatever work you do, *you* feel proud of your accomplishments and *you* feel

happy about the way of life you've chosen.

Begin every day with a promise to yourself that you will make yourself proud, and then follow through on that promise. This will help you put your abilities to use in a gentle fashion. You'll build reserves of ability and demonstrate your abilities gently and quietly but with certainty.

Another essential piece of advice I have for you is to set a clear, long-term goal. For example, a goal of gaining someone's recognition as quickly as possible is fleeting and futile. Pursuing short-term recognition is the biggest pitfall that a strongly self-assertive person can fall into, and it's a risk that can lead to a self-destructive life. Instead, your goals should focus on long-term prospects that you can dedicate yourself to for a continuous period of time.

This mindset can be likened to that of a marathon runner. When the goal is to run a very long distance, any opinions or remarks that people offer along the way just don't matter, because your focus is on keeping your pace and getting steadily closer to the finish line. Strongly self-assertive people are more apt to think like

short-distance runners. And while that kind of thinking succeeds at times, more often than not, the success is short-lived. So the key to conquering your struggles with excessive self-assertiveness is to think like a marathon runner instead of a sprinter.

5

"I Feel Trapped in the Past"

The Key to Healing the Past Is to Look to a Positive Future

It can be difficult to manage feelings of being trapped in the past. People grieve their past for any number of reasons, and it may seem impracticable to look for a solution that fits them all. But the essence of this problem is quite simple: it's the tendency to brood over the past.

We humans are interesting beings: we each perceive and understand reality differently. Take the case of how we respond to something as simple as a rainy day. Some people find rainy weather refreshing and pleasant, while others are dismayed by it or completely resent it. We also see varying perceptions in more serious situations, such as being admonished by a superior: while one subordinate may take an admonishment as a sign of the boss's high expectations, another may take it to mean that she is not competent enough to do her job.

In the majority of cases, an experience of deep pain in childhood or youth is creating this tendency to feel trapped in the past. The hurt lives on inside.

As these examples show, people can perceive the same situations in very different ways, which begs the question of how our different perceptions ultimately lead to different life outcomes.

In the majority of cases, an experience of deep pain in childhood or youth is creating this tendency to feel trapped in the past. The hurt lives on inside. Many situations can lead to enduring psychological pain: a serious illness, being born into poverty, a parent's abandonment, having a brother or sister with special needs, failing to get into college, flunking a grade, going through a difficult breakup, and being laid off from a job are all examples of such experiences. These kinds of unhappy experiences may leave behind deep pain that doesn't easily go away, and this pain can strongly affect people's lives. The pain is like a wound that is covered most of the time but that, by dint of some catalyst or other, becomes opened again so that the person ends up reliving the earlier pain. Based on my observations, a considerable number of people fall into this self-destructive pattern.

The wound needs the proper treatment to heal, and the proper way to heal inner pain is not by brooding over it for years. If you keep focusing on the hurt, the wound can never heal. But if you stop dwelling in the past and instead choose to adopt a positive attitude toward life, you will begin to take much less notice of the past.

> The solution is simply to stop looking backward and firmly set your eyes forward on the road in front of you.

If you are in this predicament, you probably feel as though your life has reached an impasse on the course of growth and progress. But the truth is that you have been the one allowing yourself to keep looking behind you and thinking to yourself, "I should have done *this* back then. Why didn't I think of doing *that*, that time?" The solution is simply to stop looking backward and firmly set your eyes forward on the road in front of you. The most effective way of healing the pain and changing your tendency to brood is to begin by practicing a positive attitude and believing in a bright future.

The Three Positive Mindsets for Cultivating a Bright Outlook

Now you understand that inner pain is healed by fostering feelings of hope and thinking positively about the future. So what can you do to help yourself live with hope and a positive mindset? I would like to prescribe three solutions.

> My advice is to repeat to yourself as often as possible each day, "I *will* be successful."

My first prescription is to cultivate a sense of success. You need to feel certain that destiny will open the doors for you and that you will absolutely succeed. If, on the other hand, you allow your thoughts to carry a sense of failure, then failure will eventually manifest itself. So my advice is to repeat to yourself as often as possible each day, "I *will* be successful. I *will* achieve greatness. I *will* fulfill my destiny."

My second prescription is to believe that this world is teeming with people who want to help you succeed and that everyone is subconsciously your supporter. You need to believe that many people in this world want to collaborate with you and that your success therefore depends on putting your ideas out into the world to attract these supporters. If you are fearful of becoming a victim to people who will judge you, hurt you, and put you down, it will be difficult for the future to open its doors. The most important element of your healing and success is a conviction within yourself that by talking to people and opening your heart to them, you will attract those who subconsciously want to cooperate to help you succeed.

My third prescription is to emphasize life's positive things and take negative things with a grain of salt. This, again, is essentially about your attitude. Changing your mindset is the most crucial aspect of your healing. People who dwell on the past are apt to make mountains out of molehills. They remember bad things for a very long time but immediately forget about good things. They dismiss good fortune

as a coincidence or a fluke or even regard it as a portent of imminent misfortune.

In this modern age, fewer and fewer people are able to hold onto joy for extended lengths of time. Nowadays, most people truly struggle to take delight in the simple joys of life, and even when they do, their happiness seems to vanish quickly and be replaced by waves of unhappiness. It is now much easier to wallow in unhappiness, which ends up inviting even more unhappiness, than it is to dwell in enduring happiness.

For example, let us say that your friend said something that offended you today. The simple truth is that sometimes you don't know what really causes people to behave as they do. The insult may have felt offensive enough for the pain to linger one to two months, or perhaps even two to three years. But if you consider for a moment that your friend may have been having a bad day because of not feeling well, facing workplace struggles, or dealing with family problems, you'll realize that the insult may simply have been an impulsive, thoughtless reaction to your friend's inner frustration. Your friend probably didn't really mean to insult you

and probably will have forgotten about it tomorrow.

In this situation, I am certain that you will agree that it is unnecessary to carry around hurt feelings for months or years. As this example illustrates, we create the realities we see, and what we believe to be reality may not be the way things really are.

> You must choose the thought patterns that bring you positive results and outcomes.

My advice is to become more self-serving in the positive sense of the word. By this I mean that you must choose the thought patterns that bring you positive results and outcomes. Take negative situations—unpleasantries, ill omens, adversity, and grief—as lightly as possible. Meanwhile, take all delightful events as positively as possible, and carry them in your heart for as long as you can. This way, you will allow happiness into your life day after day.

There will be times when someone's slander or insult may hurt you. But the hurt may only last for a short period of time.

Whatever the person has said, it is probably not something that a lot of people are saying about you all the time. In fact, many people probably think well of you, and you should remind yourself of that to help you remember that you have positive aspects, as well. The key is to find ways to minimize your feelings of misery while at the same time magnifying feelings of happiness.

To sum up my prescription for those who feel trapped by the past, my advice is to change your mindset about the future into thoughts that give you hope. First, cultivate a sense of certainty that you are bound for success. Second, believe fully that those around you are your subconscious supporters. And third, pay less attention to the unhappy situations life brings, and instead maximize your focus on cultivating attitudes that bring happiness into your life.

6

"I Have a Hard Time Fitting In"

Offset Feelings of Inferiority with Ready Conversation Topics

There are probably more people than we realize who struggle to fit in in social settings. Most of the time, these are people who don't mix well with large groups of people, prefer to be by themselves, or often feel left out or ostracized. When we closely examine these people, we will find something they all have in common. They struggle with an inferiority complex regarding, for example, their personality, physical appearance, or level of intelligence. Whatever the reason may be, their inferiority complex almost always gives rise to feelings of self-consciousness—the hope that others won't notice their weaknesses.

You may have an image of them as characteristically shy, introverted people. But some of them can become especially talkative and boastful when they are around others. Their true personality is introverted, and they delight in quiet ruminations alone. But they become very voluble when they find themselves in social settings. When they return home, they often feel very embarrassed and regretful about how they behaved, and they gradually begin to avoid social activities.

There are also people who become very shy and quiet in social settings. These people might, for example, feel self-conscious about their education or intelligence, embarrassed about their lisp, or uncomfortable around people of the opposite

gender. I would like to offer the following advice to these people.

First, the majority of people are not so unkind or so mean-spirited as to try to make you feel embarrassed about your lisp or whatever it is that you feel self-conscious about. Perhaps it won't go totally unnoticed, but it's highly unlikely that they would ridicule you.

> The main reasons for your shyness are your inability to join in on conversational topics that you aren't familiar with and your fear of embarrassing yourself.

Second, if you are afraid to speak in front of people because you fear being perceived as an unintelligent person, then you may need to make an effort to change. If you really have nothing to talk about, then you can't blame others when they recognize that; the problem lies in your lack of effort. You probably haven't made an effort to become sociable because of your desire to protect yourself from embarrassment and your hope that by staying silent, you'll be perceived in a positive light.

My prescription for those who face this struggle is to prepare conversational topics that you'll be able to talk about when you are in social settings. The main reasons for your shyness are your inability to join in on conversational topics that you aren't familiar with and your fear of embarrassing yourself by saying something completely off the mark. You can easily solve this problem by educating yourself by reading books and watching movies and TV programs about trending topics. Being prepared with ready-to-go conversation topics will help you feel relaxed in your interactions with others and will help you feel less left out. This is something that can be accomplished through effort.

Open Yourself to Different People and Take the Initiative to Engage

Some people are unable to relate at all to the kinds of conversations that happen in social settings. These people often have a serious character; regard themselves as refined, studious, philosophical, and well-read intellectuals; and feel that gambling, drinking, and gossiping are beneath them. They pride themselves on their refinement and superiority over others.

I encourage such people to realize that they are still uncultivated in areas they haven't given their attention to. They have created a veneer of superiority out of a desire to protect themselves and a lack of empathy for others.

If your personality fits this description, then the reason you have difficulty fitting in arises from a lack of curiosity about other people, which is probably exacerbated by feelings of superiority and a condescending attitude. You probably feel that your understanding of life and this world is far superior to that of those around you and that you therefore don't belong with them.

But on the flip side of these feelings are probably feelings of insecurity and a desire to protect your pride. Perhaps you don't want others to judge you for being unique. Or perhaps you haven't cultivated enough understanding of human diversity and aren't able to see that all people are remarkable, no matter who they are. In effect, your behavior is confirming that you are incapable of freely and flexibly speaking and interacting with diverse groups of people.

One of the important things speakers like myself need to do is offer teachings that fit the needs of our audiences and the individuals in front of us. The mark of true cultivation and understanding is the ability to offer teachings that suit the wants of many varied individuals. So if you can give talks or lectures to audiences of people who resemble you but are unable to speak to people with different traits and characteristics, it may be a sign that you need to further cultivate your spiritual understanding. There is much more to

human beings than you currently see, and so much more to learn about.

> Create more room
> in your heart to accept
> different types of people.

It's also important to develop true confidence in yourself and to open your heart to greater acceptance of people. Create more room in your heart to accept different types of people. Ultimately, this is the secret to being able to converse with a variety of people.

If you can talk comfortably about advanced topics but falter when the unpleasant, nastier subjects of everyday life are brought up, that is a flaw that you can address. You should cultivate enough human capacity to be able to talk with people about whatever topic they bring up.

So if you have difficulty connecting with others, it is a mistake to blame it on their faults and to cherish your own feeling of superiority. What you need to do most is stand back, observe yourself humbly, and realize that you still lack learning and spiritual cultivation.

7

"People Don't Trust Me"

Do You Have a Reputation for Double-Dealing?

This case of the unhappiness syndrome may also be quite difficult to deal with. Issues with earning people's trust can arise in various kinds of situations, which makes it difficult to come up with a prescription that can solve all of them. That being said, we may be able to gain a better understanding of the general underlying causes by examining some common situations.

One thing I advise all people who face this problem to do is give their own personality a good, hard look. The reasons people don't trust you are most likely to be found in your own behavior. What you may discover, as you examine your personality, is a tendency to *not* be consciously aware of your

thinking and behavior. Thus, the main problem may be a lack of perspective about yourself.

> The reasons people don't trust you are most likely to be found in your own behavior.

The most typical reason people distrust us is that our behavior is deceptive or we are suspected of being two-faced. When our deception is detected, trust inevitably disappears. A common example is when people think that we have ulterior motives for trying to get closer to someone or that we say things we don't truly

think or feel. People can behave this way even without consciously intending to.

We often find this problem in romantic relationships when one of the partners is able to juggle multiple relationships. When a woman finds out that her boyfriend has been cheating on her, of course it is only natural for her trust in him to vanish. But what is rather interesting is that the man is often completely oblivious to the reason the woman no longer trusts him. For example, someone with this pattern of behavior may feel that he is only being honest with himself and following his heart, and he may not be able to understand why it is wrong to find all three of his girlfriends wonderful people to be with. He may believe that it's only natural to be unable to choose between them and to want to spend time with each of them on a different day of the week. He may be sincerely unable to understand why one of his girlfriends would be upset that he has been dating other women and wants to break up with him.

When we look closely at this type of behavior, we will find that he has not considered the situation from the other person's point of view. Often, he is convinced of his superior attractiveness and believes that he deserves to be treated differently than others. He approaches all his relationships based on this premise. But this is a recipe for disaster that will eventually result in his relationships falling apart at one point or other.

Do You Have a Reputation for Changing Your Opinions?

Another common behavior that we notice in this version of the unhappiness syndrome is when a person's ideas or opinions appear to frequently change. This pattern of behavior occurs mainly because of the changes in the person's mood and the way he or she happens to feel at the time. But because these frequent oscillations in mood and emotion result in frequent changes in what the person says, other people can't help but stop trusting him or her.

My advice for someone with this pattern of behavior is to determine which matters are important and which are less

significant. Then, make it a rule to explain your decisions about the important matters to the people who are involved. Clearly explain your decisions before you start acting on them.

To handle matters that are much less significant or are trivial, it's wise to let others know about your moody personality. This is probably the only way to deal with this issue. Do the best you can to explain to others that you have a tendency to change your opinions frequently but that you are essentially a good-natured person.

Do You Have a Reputation for Failing?

A third type of behavior that often gives rise to this syndrome is a habit of failure or incompetency at work. If you find this pattern in yourself, you may feel frustrated that your superiors or colleagues don't trust you, but the problem lies in your own tendency to make mistakes when you're given a job to handle. This is actually a very common problem that many people face.

What is happening in this situation is that people are avoiding giving you jobs out of fear that doing so may ultimately lead to mistakes or failure. Meanwhile, you resent not being trusted.

My advice is to find and analyze the reason people don't trust you instead of resenting the situation. You should discover that the real problem is your lack of proper working skills and methods. This is the issue you need to address. To do so, closely examine the methods you have been using to carry out your work and look for ways to improve on them. To get ideas for how you might improve, closely study the working methods of colleagues and superiors who are recognized for their competence. You can also ask them for direct advice.

What a lot of people in this predicament tend to do is try to appear confident by making big promises. Then they find themselves in trouble when they can't fulfill their promise. If this often happens to you, the solution is to stop putting on airs; don't make huge promises you won't be able to fulfill. Instead, focus on what you are capable of doing and do

those things surely and steadily. Put your energy into making the effort to accrue smaller successes.

When you feel you are being judged as incompetent, your anger may get the best of you, and you may react by trying to accomplish something big in an effort to prove your competence. But this will most likely result in disastrous outcomes, and in turn it will make people trust you less than ever. In these circumstances, rather than trying to expand the scope of your work too widely, it's much wiser to keep it within reasonable bounds and work to build your accomplishments from there. Once you have accomplished enough within a limited scope, you will be ready to move onto further areas of work. There are times when what seems like pulling back leads to expanded possibilities in the future. This means that it's important to consider whether your current circumstances are such that taking one step backward could ultimately move you two steps forward.

> Focus on what you are capable of doing and do those things surely and steadily. Put your energy into making the effort to accrue smaller successes.

Do You Have a Reputation for Divulging Information?

A fourth reason for losing others' trust is an inability to keep information confidential. Some people have loose lips and are prone to allowing information to slip into their conversations.

Many circumstances require us to handle information with a certain degree of confidentiality. People often talk to each other or share information based on a premise of trust. They trust that the information will be handled with care and respect. But if someone shares something with you under the assumption of

privacy and then finds out that many other people know about it, it's only natural for that person to lose trust in you and decide to never confide in you again.

If this is a trait that you have, my advice is to learn how to better determine the kinds of information that should be kept private or confidential. Also, if someone comes to you to discuss a personal problem and asks that you keep it to yourself, but you feel that you may inadvertently let it slip out, then I recommend cautioning the person beforehand. You can simply explain that you have a difficult time keeping matters completely confidential and ask not to be told anything that shouldn't be mentioned to anyone else.

Some people will still want to talk to you about everything. You can't always avoid people's confidences, and the kind thing to do is to be their friend and listen. They probably need someone to talk to to help them feel better and get things off their chest. In these situations, it's wise to be as careful as possible about keeping your friend's personal matters to yourself.

That said, the best principle to follow is to refrain from being a confidant if you have a talkative personality that makes you prone to handling sensitive information poorly. If you don't have a talkative personality, then it may be safe for people to trust you. But if you are naturally a talkative person who easily shares people's personal matters with others, then you might make your friend's problems worse by accidentally violating their confidence. The wisest course to take in that case is to keep clear of other people's secretive or private matters as best as you can.

A related trait, the tendency to be very talkative about one's own private or confidential matters, can also lead people to distrust you. You don't have to be completely open about yourself to build trusting friendships. As the proverb goes, "A hedge between keeps friendships green." Good friendships need a degree of mutual respect and it's not always constructive to be so open. To build trusting friendships, it's very important to show your friends your positive qualities.

8

"I Don't Have Confidence in My Intelligence"

Schools Measure Scholastic Achievement

With the high value we put on intelligence these days, more and more people suffer from a lack of confidence in their intelligence. But how do we measure intelligence? Studies have shown that not all people who were at the top of their class in high school and college went on to create successful careers for themselves. When we start to work in the real world, our personality can influence our success more than our ability to score high on exams does. So those who performed well academically may have gained the respect of many of their peers at the time, but they may be struggling to succeed in the working world if their personality is prone to be downcast and withdrawn. These outcomes show that your grades in school are not necessarily full indications of your true capabilities. This is an essential point to keep in mind in our understanding of intelligence.

> Your grades in school are not necessarily full indications of your true capabilities.

In this section, I offer separate advice for those who are still students and those who have finished school and are working on their careers. I start with my advice to students. Students' job is to further their education, and they're under constant pressure to score well on the many exams that the educational system mandates. They are probably struggling to

deal with the emotional highs and lows of a demanding academic life.

When we think of how intelligence is commonly measured, we mostly think of IQ tests, standardized achievement tests, and grades in school. But these methods are chiefly indications of our level of academic achievement, rather than purely our intelligence.

What do these measures of academic achievement really mean? Our scores on standardized achievement tests essentially measure our academic achievements through high school. This means that these scores are chiefly a measure of our academic performance over a fixed span of about twelve years or so. The aim of scholastic education is to raise our academic performance to a certain, expected level, and each student is competing to perform better than the others.

What happens when we take this span of time entirely out of this equation? If we compare a student who is majoring in a foreign language with a professional interpreter with ten, twenty, or thirty years of experience, the language proficiency and capability of the student will have no chance against that of the professional interpreter. So as a student, it is crucial to know that the intelligence that most people refer to in the context of academic education is referring to our ability to perform at a certain scholastic level within a limited time span.

Improve Your Efficiency and Memory to Do Better in School

So what can we do to reach a certain level of academic performance within a specific span of time? There are two ways to do this.

The first way is to improve our efficiency. Efficiency is crucial, because we are expected to absorb a lot of information in many subjects within a fixed period of time. This means that improving our grades depends largely on getting the most out of every hour we have available to study. So if your study skills have remained very crude, you are most likely to get unsatisfactory results.

The efficient study methods we cultivate through our academic education will continue to be very useful when we become a working member of society. The reason why many large corporations recruit new graduates with a strong record of academic achievement is that these students' efficient study habits will translate into efficient work performance. In this sense, the study habits and methods that you develop in school will be advantageous in your career.

Knowledge can make a difference not only in the depth of thinking we give to our work and the decisions we make, but also in the intellectual richness and fulfillment we gain from life.

The second way of improving academic performance is to develop our memorization skills. Schools often heavily emphasize our ability to memorize a large amount of information. Our ability to memorize information is at its prime during our teens and begins to gradually decline

after our twenties. So one of our essential missions during our early years is to learn and remember as much information as possible while our memories are still strong and active. There are significant benefits of developing a strong memory, so we shouldn't overlook the advantages we gain from an education that emphasizes memorization.

There are two main benefits of developing a strong memory. First, a strong memory allows us to gather a larger amount of information to serve as our basis for thinking and decision making. Why is gathering knowledge an important aspect of our success? Knowledge can make a difference not only in the depth of thinking we give to our work and the decisions we make, but also in the intellectual richness and fulfillment we gain from life.

For example, someone with a strong base of knowledge about world and American history is much better qualified to think through many work matters than is someone with a weak knowledge-base in this area. Someone with a background in history will be able to consider how George Washington, Abraham Lincoln, General Grant, and General Lee would have approached a problem and analyze the problem from these different perspectives. What we know about these historical figures can deepen the level of analysis and thought that we are able to put into the matters we handle, and this depth of thinking will clearly be different from someone who doesn't know much about these figures.

> The years we spend in school are the groundwork that will allow us to perform our jobs efficiently and well when we begin working after we graduate.

The second benefit of developing a strong memory is that it effectively doubles our capabilities or, more specifically, our brainpower or intellectual capability. Just as we strengthen our muscles through regular exercise and training, we strengthen our intellect through use and practice. For example, let's compare the intellects of ancient peoples to the intellects of people living today. Compared with the intellectual capacity that was possible

when civilizations were mainly agricultural societies that focused on physical work, the intellectual capacity of modern people who are living and working in an age of advanced information is going to be far superior. So it is important to know that a strong intellect can be developed through effort.

What this all means is that we shouldn't regard studying for exams as a meaningless waste of time. The years we spend in school are the groundwork that will allow us to perform our jobs efficiently and well when we begin working after we graduate. In addition, the strong memorization skills that school life demands provide vital intellectual training. The memorization abilities that we develop in school build a tough brain that can endure long hours of focused concentration. So for all these reasons, the efforts we make to improve our exam scores has valuable meaning to our lives.

Based on our discussion so far, we can say that those who struggle at school are either using inefficient study methods or have weak memories. You will need to determine which of these is your main problem.

My advice to those who are studying inefficiently is to come

up with new ways of using their time more efficiently and to keep aiming for improvement.

My advice to those who are struggling to improve their memory is to put effort into improving their concentration skills. By training your mind to keep it focused, your memory will improve. Put another way, you can greatly improve your memory by training your mind to stop being distracted by other things.

One aspect of a good memory is the ability to retain information for a long span of time. This skill isn't as important in the context of education because the span of time we need to remember information is quite limited. On the other hand, a scattered, easily distracted mind will make it hard to focus on absorbing information and will inhibit your academic performance in the long run. So in this situation, it's more important to be able to focus our attention on our studies for a long time than it is to retain information for a long time.

The value of the power to concentrate becomes all the more clear when we begin working. When we get a job, we are expected to work eight to ten hours a day on tasks that are not necessarily exciting. What this requires is perseverance, and perseverance requires the ability to concentrate on our job. The ability to persevere throughout the day depends on how well we can keep concentrating on the task at hand. If we tend to be easily distracted, it's that much harder to do our job well.

Another way to improve your memory is by simply putting more time into practicing memorization. The basic principle that the intelligent should use wisdom and the not-so-intelligent should use sweat holds true in the context of building our memory. If your memory isn't as quick to absorb information as others who may be able to commit things to memory in two or three reads, you will probably still be able to absorb a lot of information by reading the same thing five to ten times. There are basically only two ways to improve memory: use efficient methods and techniques or use sweat and labor. So if you feel that you aren't particularly clever, your option is to go over the same things with more frequency.

Heredity influences intelligence to some degree, so your effort probably won't result in a sudden, extraordinary leap in your

level of intelligence. But if, let's say, your current level of intelligence was at one hundred points, it is absolutely possible to improve that by twenty to thirty points through effort. It isn't realistic to expect to reach five hundred or one thousand points quickly, but we all have the potential to improve our intelligence by about twenty to thirty percent.

Eventually, if you keep up this kind of improvement for ten to twenty years, the time will come when you will eventually surpass someone at a level of five hundred points. This is a self-evident principle. Simple math shows that if we set your current intelligence at one hundred points, then there is a four-hundred-point difference between you and someone at five hundred points. This means that if we estimate your improvement in intelligence to be twenty points each year, then you will be able to catch up to this person in twenty years.

Even if someone currently has five times your level of intelligence, if you persist in your efforts, you will eventually outperform this person. Limiting yourself to a span of three to four years may not let you accomplish

this, but if you extend that and think of it as a long-term goal, you will open yourself up to the possibility of a complete turn-around in your success.

> If you keep up this kind of improvement for ten to twenty years, the time will come when you will eventually surpass someone at a level of five hundred points.

For those who find themselves unable to improve their academic performance even after putting in effort, I recommend focusing on putting effort into other areas of your work when you get your first job after graduation. Your personality and character are vital elements of success, and this is also an area in which you can cultivate a mental toughness. Doing so is another way of enhancing your potential to succeed. Those with vitality and the ability to take action and make decisions will also come to be known for their intelligence as their record of accomplishment grows.

Absorb the Wisdom and Skills of Superior People

Now I would like to offer advice to those who are already in the working world. There are probably many working people who are not confident in their intelligence. Usually, they are struggling with poor job performance.

This problem arises chiefly from the slack attitude they put into their education. It's absurd to expect that by neglecting to work hard at school, you will somehow be able to perform well at work. It doesn't work this way, because most jobs require a lot of paperwork. Working with documents requires attention to detail as well as the ability to make decisions efficiently and process the documents properly. When you are unable to do well in school, it often translates into an inability to work with documents in the workplace. Unfortunately, if you try to use your stamina to compensate for your lack of skill, you'll usually end up spending a lot of time on each document, so your efficiency suffers.

There is no use wallowing in the past however, so if you are in this situation, I recommend borrowing wisdom and skills from people who are more capable and competent than you are. In other words, I recommend cultivating the skills and abilities that you currently lack.

Persistence is power. This is the key. Find a role model that you believe is far more exceptional, intelligent, and capable than you are and who also has an outstanding character, and read that person's books or written work for at least an hour every day. This is truly the only way to improve your job performance.

> I recommend borrowing wisdom and skills from people who are more capable and competent than you are.

Keep absorbing your chosen role model's words, and keep learning from them. By cultivating yourself in this manner, you will learn to develop insightful perspectives on your work, your administrative efficiency will

improve, and you will also begin to read office documents more quickly.

This brings up another piece of advice I have, and that is to increase the speed at which you read. Often, those who struggle with their intelligence are slow readers. The job performance of someone who reads quickly will obviously be much better than that of someone who reads very slowly. So training yourself to read more quickly is another vital way to improve your intelligence. Even just this one improvement can help you feel more efficient and intelligent, and it will also give you some breathing room. I hope you will continue to come up with ways to enhance your capabilities and create some elbow room for yourself as well.

9

"I Have High Aspirations, but They Feel Impossible to Reach"

Set an Aspiration to Hold On to for Three Years

All of us go through a time, at least once in our life, when we feel frustrated that we're not achieving our aspirations. The star college athlete dreams of being drafted by a professional team, and a great many young people aspire to be of benefit to the world. But over time, we often let these aspirations shrink until they become much smaller than they were originally.

Let's consider the example of a college student from a rural area who is admitted to a distinguished university. It's a huge challenge for a student from a rural area to gain admission into a top-ranking university, so that is a tremendous achievement in itself. This student feels very proud of his accomplishment and embarks

on his freshman year with high hopes and aspirations, confident that he has earned this chance to achieve greatness and leave his mark on history. But when he arrives on campus and goes to orientation, what really awaits him is the shocking reality that there are thousands of other students just like himself. What's more shocking is realizing how unlikely it would be for every student there to become a great achiever or a rare genius. The reality that sets in is much more severe and challenging than the student had expected. Until this moment, he hadn't questioned his worth, but now it feels as though his importance has been taken from him in one fell swoop. Suddenly, he feels ordinary and trifling.

The same basic principle holds true when we begin our career after graduation. In Japan, it is common for all newly graduated employees to begin with very basic jobs, such as filing, staffing the copy machine, and doing other menial tasks around the office. Someone who gets scouted by a highly distinguished company may have hopes of working hard and contributing great things to the company. By contrast, the reality of first-year employee work may feel disenchanting.

Many Japanese companies offer employees opportunities to study abroad. But when an employee proudly returns with an MBA from an American university, she may find herself relegated to translation jobs instead of the larger projects she was hoping to be entrusted with.

As these examples show, even when we believe we've accomplished something that should earn us a chance to put our abilities to use, it is actually very common to face disenchanting realities that can alienate us from our aspirations.

What can we do when our dreams break down and real life doesn't offer us an opportunity to put our abilities to the test?

I advise setting a goal or aspiration that you are certain you can hold onto for at least three years. What most people consider to be high aspirations are very frail in reality—too delicate to last more than one or two months, or perhaps six months at the most. High aspirations aren't truly aspirations at all if they are that fragile; in that case, they really only should be considered big dreams.

> If you can continue for three years without giving up, that will be an extraordinary accomplishment in itself.

So set a real aspiration that you can work toward for at least three years. If you can continue for three years without giving up, that will be an extraordinary accomplishment in itself. When you achieve your aspiration, you can use your achievement as a stepping-stone to inspire you toward your next dream.

The truth about having big dreams is that, most of the time, they cannot be achieved immediately. Furthermore, often we

won't have a chance to realize our dreams until we have reached a certain position in our career or profession.

Today, I am able to make many of my dreams reality largely due to my position as the founder and CEO of Happy Science Group. I was unable to make many of them come true, no matter how strongly I wished for them, until I reached this position. When you think about it, our environment is in a state of constant change, year after year. This essentially means that we won't be the same person three years down the road. This is another reason I emphasize the importance of choosing an aspiration that you can hold onto continuously for three years and to begin that journey now.

Your True Talents Lie Hidden within Your Interests

My next piece of advice is for those who are unsure of what aspirations they should set for themselves. If this is you, ask yourself this question: "What is the one thing I am most interested in or am most eagerly drawn to?" Our true talents are hidden within the areas of interest that our hearts are most strongly drawn to.

No matter how often you go on hiking trips, you will find them hard to enjoy it if what you are really interested in is swimming. Likewise, if you are strongly drawn to learning Spanish but are forcing yourself to study architectural design instead, you are not likely to derive a deep sense of fulfilment from your studies. Whereas, if what you love to do is to swim, simply spending more time swimming will allow your talent to eventually blossom. The ability to have an interest is a talent in itself.

So I recommend that you begin by choosing an area of interest that you truly love and spending ample time delving into it. Perhaps it's playing a sport, learning a new language, learning a new subject, or simply having a hobby. It can be anything, as long as you are fascinated by it and can continue being absorbed in it for three consecutive years. After three years of putting effort into it and building some degree

of confidence, you will reach a level that is very close to that of a professional or at least a semi-professional in the field.

I recommend that you begin by choosing an area of interest that you truly love.

The next step I recommend is widening your horizons and expanding your areas of interest. The human mind is naturally inclined to seek a wide range of interests, which makes it difficult to limit ourselves to just one area of interest throughout our entire life. So once you have become strong in one area, it is important to think about how you would like to expand your interests into other areas. This will allow you to widen your capacity.

Those who make continuous efforts in any area will be blessed by an opportunity to put their talent to use at some point, and that will in turn bring further progress to their lives.

Put more simply, the vital point is essentially this: we need to put in the effort if we wish to open up possible paths to our dreams and aspirations. The prerequisite for the realization of our dreams and aspirations is our effort. Of course, there will be times when the doors to our dreams never seem to open, no matter how much work we put into them. In this case, the question is how long you will be able to patiently persevere. It is only very rarely that our effort is not rewarded in our lifetime. And even if our effort goes unrewarded before our time here is up, then I am certain we will be recognized by future generations.

The question is how long you will be able to patiently persevere.

For example, some writers of the past are now highly regarded throughout the world but only gained this recognition posthumously. As long as we continue to make the effort to make our souls shine forth, the time will eventually come when this effort is brought to light. What is most vital is to believe this to be true and to never cease working on the things we love.

10

"I Can't Stop Thinking Pessimistically"

Pessimistic Thinking Is an Instinctive Reaction to Fear

Life brings us suffering as well as joy, and we all go through times when we cannot seem to lift ourselves out of a bleak, pessimistic outlook on life. When everything you do seems to be going wrong, it can feel impossible or unrealistic to live optimistically and carefree, no matter how much you are encouraged to do so. Perhaps these are the times when we keenly realize that we are psychological creatures.

To illustrate how to combat this pattern of negative thinking, I would first like to examine the nature of pessimistic thinking. If you have a consistent pattern of feeling defeated, hesitant, and reluctant and are convinced that everything that you do is likely to fail, then you need to stand back and realize that you are currently in a state of deep self-absorption. Even if your pessimism could simply be due to a lack of success, the fact still remains that your suffering is arising from a strong focus on protecting yourself. Some people are so absorbed with fear that they go through life paranoid about the possibility of an asteroid hitting them as they are walking outside.

Our tendency to predict negative outcomes arises from our basic animal instinct to detect danger in our surroundings. We can see this in cats as they poise themselves to immediately run away at the sight of someone approaching them. This happens all by instinct. They watch our movements very carefully and run off as soon as they sense a threat. Dogs also have this trait. They may see someone who comes into the house as a potential threat to their and their family's safety, so they will bark very loudly or crouch down in preparation to lunge and bite if necessary. Mice also always seem to be prepared to detect danger and run away immediately.

Sensing threats is the main focus of an animal's mind because animals are constantly exposed to predators from which they need to protect themselves night and day to survive. Their second focus is to procure food, another necessity for survival. The human tendency to think pessimistically and expect unfavorable outcomes closely resembles this animal instinct.

Pessimistic thinking can be likened to the fear reaction of a fish that has almost been caught by the bait on a fishing line. It's said that fish that have experienced this won't be able to eat anything for a while due to the fear they've developed. Human beings react in similar ways to certain situations. If we've been deceived before by

an opportunity that seemed to offer many benefits, we may have developed a suspicion of all opportunities that sound beneficial.

Our tendency to predict negative outcomes arises from our basic animal instinct to detect danger in our surroundings.

There may be times when this apprehension may feel so strong that we are no longer capable of believing in good opportunities, and we allow ourselves to choose failure of our own volition. As ironic as this behavior may seem, this is a very common cause of suffering. For example, if you have been through several steady relationships that you were sure would blossom into marriage, but all of them ended with your partner breaking up with you, you may develop a fear of rejection. Then, even when you finally find a partner who sincerely wishes to marry you, the fear from your past relationships may cause you to react by being the one to initiate the breakup, all because of your fear of another rejection.

Then after a few days, you will probably come to your senses and regret your mistake.

I've seen this pattern of unhappiness in many people. So why does it happen? This is a case in which you've experienced failure so often that it has essentially become ingrained in your subconscious. In other words, you have developed a pattern of expecting failure all the time. Since you are now afraid of feeling hurt any further, you subconsciously react by initiating the failure yourself.

> You have developed a pattern of expecting failure all the time.

Another example of the influence of fear underlying pessimistic thinking can be seen in students who regularly fall ill with a stomach virus, headache, or fever come midterms and final exams. This phenomenon also has a subconscious cause. We humans are capable of developing ill symptoms in our subconscious minds that then become manifested physically. This happens when we become afraid of taking exams for fear of horrible results; we are afraid of disappointing ourselves. We subconsciously hope that by falling ill we will have an excuse if we do poorly on the exam.

We can also observe a pattern of pessimistic thinking in people who develop neurosis or a nervous disorder. A very large number of people these days are suffering from this problem, and it is working against their happiness. Ever since medicine discovered the existence of nerves throughout our bodies, we've seen a drastic increase in people who are diagnosed with nervous disorders. Many unexplainable illnesses tend to be diagnosed as nervous disorders based on the idea that our nervous system can become weakened and diseased and that this creates the anxiety and inner suffering that we feel.

But this idea will result in placing the fault for our unhappiness on external circumstances. Since nerves are our organs' means of communication with one another, it is flawed to think that our nerves have the ability to create feelings of anxiety. The real cause of problems with anxiety lies in past experiences of hurt and pain that we want to protect ourselves

from experiencing again. For example, someone who has been badly burned by touching a hot pan may become very afraid of touching pots and pans without oven mitts to protect their hands. Many people suffer from this type of fear, which is very well-described by the proverb "Once bitten, twice shy."

Find Seeds of Joy and Spend Less Time on Negative Thoughts

My prescription for healing patterns of pessimistic thinking can be summed up into two steps.

First, decrease the amount of time that you spend wallowing in negative thoughts. People who suffer from pessimistic thinking often find their minds filled with thoughts and images of their failures. Sometimes they may suddenly realize that they've been replaying their past words over and over in their mind.

I recommend telling yourself how important it is to move on and forget your failures after you have allowed yourself to think about them once. So, each time a negative thought enters your mind, get rid of it immediately and stop thinking about it. Turn this into your new habit and cultivate this positive version of forgetfulness. Just as your pattern of pessimistic thinking was developed by habit, the ability to forget and let go can also be learned by habit. It will become much easier with practice.

> Each time a negative thought enters your mind, get rid of it immediately.

Second, infuse your mind with positive thoughts. Many things in your daily surroundings can give you a sense of simple joy. So in addition to learning to stop your negative thoughts, you also need to proactively search around you to find these seeds of joy. For example, when you come home from a difficult day at work feeling downbeat and frustrated, look for the things in your home life that bring you joy. If your spouse, who finds cooking to be a challenge, has prepared you a sumptuous,

satisfying dinner, it's the perfect chance to compliment and thank your spouse for such a delicious meal and for being such a wonderful partner. This will not only bring a smile to your spouse's face, but will lift your spirits as well.

> You can find countless seeds of happiness lying all around you if you make an effort to notice them.

You can find countless seeds of happiness lying all around you if you make an effort to notice them. Paying attention to all these sources of joy will help you realize how thankful you are to be alive and how much happiness you already hold. Joy is always around us; we just haven't made the effort to notice it.

My advice is to find at least one seed of happiness every day. There is a proverb that says, "Do your good deed for the day." But even if you don't accomplish a good deed every single day, I believe that you can build a path to progress simply by finding one seed of happiness every day. By doing so, I am certain that avenues of happiness and success will open to you.

11

"I Have a Secret I Don't Want Others to Know"

Focus on Building a Bright Future Instead of Being Stuck in the Past

The truth is that everyone probably has at least one or two problems or insecurities that they have tried to hide by lying about them. Even someone who seems to have the most open, honest, and cheerful personality goes through problems in life and may have circumstances in his or her private life that are causing a lot of inward suffering.

First, it may help you to know that no one truly watches other people closely enough to figure out their secrets. For example, Miss Universe may seem to us to have a perfect, happy life. Not only does she have the attention of people around the world who respect her for her beauty and intelligence, but countless men also admire her. But in real life, she may actually have a family member who suffers from a serious illness, and trying out for the Miss Universe pageant may have been her way of getting her mind off her private suffering and giving herself a chance to be in the limelight.

Next, let's examine the reasons why we feel the need to hide things from others. The things that people most often try to hide about themselves are physical imperfections, other flaws, and past failures. Someone who has failed in his business or has been let go from a job will most likely want to hide that part of his life as much as possible. An inadequate educational or family background

is also a circumstance that many people try to hide from others.

The urge to hide or lie about our flaws arises from underlying feelings of inadequacy and insecurity. We have an emotional need to appear normal to those around us, so when we notice our flaws and imperfections, they give rise to the urge to keep them a secret or cover them up with lies. If, on the other hand, our feelings of insecurity are far outweighed by the confidence we feel about our positive attributes, then our flaws aren't a source of concern. And when we try to hide our flaws, people often detect them anyway because we spend so much of our time being concerned about them.

What I would like to ask is this: Does it truly matter whether or not people know about your past? What's far more precious to your life than your past is how wonderful and remarkable you can be in the present.

Let's say that as a child, you faced financial challenges that led to adverse circumstances throughout your childhood: you lost your parents as a small child, were raised in a foster home with very little money, and could afford a part-time college education.

Then, as a result of a lack of academic qualifications, you suffered for one or two decades in the work world because this problem held you back.

Having gone through such challenging circumstances, you might find fault with your childhood environment and blame your family's financial situation for your limited education. You might feel that the reason for your lack of success isn't a lack of inherent potential or ability, but rather society's unfair judgments and the value society places on academic history. So you feel that it's right to blame your lack of education for large corporations not hiring you or your workplace not promoting you.

It may be that your true potential is full of promise and your family circumstances didn't afford you the opportunity to receive a good education. This may be the truth, especially if you are confident in your true potential.

Yet, the fact remains that other people have little else except your academic background to help them determine your potential for success. It is not their responsibility to consider how to get around this problem for you. Nor is it the responsibility of your family and

relatives. It depends wholly on you and how you deal with these circumstances.

> What's far more precious to your life than your past is how wonderful and remarkable you can be in the present.

In fact, even if you hold a full-time job, you have many opportunities to continue your education. There are many ways to earn a degree or certifications for specialized skills. Opportunities like these can be found everywhere. So why haven't you taken advantage of these opportunities?

The reason is that you have been dwelling on your past and making it your excuse for not doing anything to improve your circumstances.

If you truly want to erase your sources of insecurity and inadequacy, then my advice is to stop wallowing in the past and using it as an excuse to fail, and instead start focusing on building a bright and hopeful future. If your insecurity comes from an inferiority complex related to your level of education, then the answer is to make the effort to further your education in a way that others will recognize. The effort you make will eventually produce results and help build your confidence.

Forget About Problems that Cannot Be Solved by Fretting

Another common source of insecurity is imperfections in our physical appearance, whether they are noticeable or unnoticeable to others. If you have a physical flaw that you can improve through effort, then by all means, make the effort to improve it. But in many cases, effort will be in vain. If this is the case, it won't help to dwell on it.

Instead, it is wiser to spend your energy on developing an area of your strength that will help compensate for your feelings of inadequacy.

Common forms of imperfection that cannot be changed are those that are determined by genetics, such as being naturally short. We can try things like taking calcium supplements to

promote our growth. But there are no methods that offer radical change. Being active in a sport can help lengthen our limbs, but the changes are subtle and don't necessarily provide the kind of results we might want. For example, people who play basketball and volleyball have found that these sports help them get somewhat taller, but the results tend to show up in their upper bodies rather than in their legs.

Since we can't change these physical imperfections no matter how hard we try, it serves no purpose to worry about being ridiculed by others or how these flaws might affect our chances of getting married. Genetic physical flaws are neither your fault nor anyone else's. Not even God can help you in this regard, and all the years that you spend fretting about them will be of no avail. The same holds true for those who have lost a limb or developed a handicap due to an accident.

Consider that each second you spend wallowing in insecurity is only working against you and laying precious time to waste. What you must do in these situations is shift your focus from your inadequacies to the positive aspects of yourself that hold potential.

Dale Carnegie, an American lecturer and New Thought author, lost a thumb as a child when he jumped out of a window and a ring he was wearing accidently got caught on a nail. He wrote about it in one of his books and said that he was only reminded of it once a month, if at all. His mind and energy were so devoted to having a constructive, positive mindset and living life to the fullest that he hardly had a moment to spend on the handicap imposed by his missing finger.

> What's more precious to life is the ideals we set for ourselves and our passion to put our all into achieving them.

In conclusion, the tendency to fret and dwell on one thing means that we are not focusing on living positively and aiming for higher goals and values. What's more precious to life is the ideals we set for ourselves and our passion to put our all into achieving them. These things allow our insecurities to become insignificant trifles.

PART III

The Unhappiness Syndrome for Women and Families

6 HABITS AND PRESCRIPTIONS FOR SOLVING MARITAL AND HOME PROBLEMS

1
"I Don't Think
My Husband Loves Me"

Women Have an Intrinsic Desire for Love

This chapter is particularly dedicated to solving problems that many women have traditionally faced. A lack of love seems to be one of the most common issues women find in their marriage lives. We can probably find millions of wives who feel unloved by their partner, and this challenge is not unique to marriage; it happens in all kinds of romantic relationships. Women are made to desire love, and that's why they feel desperate when this fundamental need is not fulfilled.

Why do women particularly seek love from their spouse or partner? The answer to this question has to do with their most basic need: survival. It has to do with the nature of marriage and family and the physiological, societal, and psychological traits typically associated with their gender.

Generally speaking, women feel more insecure when they feel unloved, because for much of human history, love has been imperative to ensuring the security of their family's lives. Imagine a world where women did not seek love from men at all. Men and women would probably fiercely compete against each other, and that competition could even escalate into an all-out-war.

Many of us decide to get married, start a family, and raise children based on the expectation that we will be nurturing a long-term, loving relationship with our spouse. Traditionally, securing love has been especially important for women during the nine-month pregnancy period, when they needed protection. We can get a sense of how vulnerable expectant mothers may have felt by looking at pregnant animals in the wild; they can easily fall prey to predators and need another animal to protect their lives. Mothers with infants and toddlers are just as vulnerable and so remain feeling insecure until their children grow up.

So that they can survive and secure protection for their children during the ten- to twenty-year period of childbearing and child-rearing, women are born with an innate desire for love or an instinctive desire for safety. If they don't feel secured and loved, it can be very difficult for them to devote a significant amount of their time to building a family and raising children.

This is why many women look for financial stability when choosing a marriage partner. Some may call those who look for high income, status, and position in their marriage partner calculating. But we should know that this trait is rooted in the desire for security and stability.

> Women tend to have a strong desire for love because of the unique and special gift they are endowed with.

Financial instability evokes a feeling of insecurity about all the years it takes to bear and raise children. Driven by the fear of insecurity, many women search for men with high incomes who can provide a strong financial base. In general, women tend to have a strong desire for love because of the unique and special gift they are endowed with.

Look at Yourself through the Eyes of Your Partner

My advice to those who lament a lack of love in their marriage is definitely not that they should keep complaining about it until they get it. Instead, it is to keep in mind that this pain is often caused by misunderstanding.

Do you take for granted that your partner should love you unconditionally, that your partner

should be attracted to you, pursue you, and adore you, no matter what? If your answer to these questions is "yes," take a moment to try to see yourself from your partner's point of view.

Let me walk you through this exercise using a hypothetical example of a married couple. Let's say a beautiful and attractive woman marries Mr. Right, who has a high income and high status and is well-built, vibrant, kind, affectionate, caring, and loving. He works very hard on the front line, and his success at his job has earned him the trust of his coworkers. He is very popular, especially with women.

Let's assume that his wife, after a while, starts to take him for granted and stops doing all the things she used to do to be attractive to him. She stops caring about the clothes she wears, does not bother to wear makeup at home, and completely neglects to take care of how she looks. Since her husband earns enough

to support the family, perhaps she has quit her job to be a home-maker. But she neglects her job as a homemaker and lets the laundry pile up for weeks, keeps the sink full of dirty dishes, and never takes out the trash, so that flies start buzzing around the kitchen.

How do you think her husband would feel when he comes home to see his wife and home like this? Do you think that he would be happy and motivated to work hard to support her and love her?

He would probably look at his wife and think, "This is ridiculous. I've just come home after long hours of hard work, and look what I get: a cluttered house, unwashed dishes in the kitchen, dirty laundry piling up on the floor, an unmade bed, and a wife who does nothing but eat and sleep."

He might believe that complaining would just invite more trouble, and he might be unable to think of a better way to communicate his unhappiness to his wife, so he might choose to become silent instead of talking things over with her. Eventually, he might come home only to eat, bathe, and sleep. As this situation continues, the wife may begin to lament a lack of love from her husband.

The problem here may simply

be that the husband has been bottling up his frustration rather than communicating openly with his wife, because he is afraid that any kind of open communication would lead to a huge fight that would make both of them even more unhappy.

Play the Role of a Delightful and Attractive Wife

If you find yourself in a situation like this, justifying your instinctive desire for love won't improve the situation. Instead, you need to see the situation from the other person's point of view and ponder what your part may be in making it difficult for your spouse to maintain feelings of love and affection for you. For example, if a woman wants a husband who will adore her and wants him to be her Prince Charming, she needs to play a role of Cinderella or Snow White. She can't play the role of the wolf from *Little Red Riding Hood* dressed in Grandma's clothes. Although lavishing love may be the husband's duty, playing the role of an attractive and lovable wife is also an important task.

If you are lamenting a lack of love from your husband, try seeing yourself through his eyes. Think about what kind of person you would find attractive if you were in your partner's shoes. It would be unfair and immature to keep demanding that your spouse be your ideal husband without first trying to see yourself objectively.

> Think about what kind of person you would find attractive if you were in your partner's shoes.

You can take the same approach if you are not happy with your sex life. Would you be drawn to you if you were your husband? Playing the role of a charming and devoted partner may make you more attractive. Learning to see yourself from the perspective of the loved one you're not happy with can help you improve your relationship.

2

"My In-Laws
Are Driving Me Crazy"

Remember, Your Parents-in-Law
Raised Your Husband

"I just can't take my intrusive and nagging mother-in-law!" is a trite complaint that we hear from many married people. The issue of not being able to get along with our in-laws is so classic that it has become an essential ingredient in the storylines of soap operas.

In olden times in many societies, marrying into a family was much harder for women because the bride was expected to accustom herself to the way things were done in the groom's family, however different they were. The ordeal the new bride had to go through must have been as painful as sleeping on a bed of thorns. However, in recent times, as women have gained more power and status, these societies have seen an increase in the number of

nuclear families that live independently of their parents. This may have helped ease the distress of dealing with challenging mothers-in-law.

> Around 70 to 80 percent of the physical and inner characteristics that define who your spouse is today are inherited from your parents-in-law.

Living as a nuclear family, away from your in-laws, is certainly one wise way to avoid conflicts, because then you simply have fewer opportunities to see one another. And if you live in a condo or apartment in a city, you probably won't have extra space to share with your parents, which automatically prevents them from living under your roof.

Living away from your in-laws has its advantages. But whether you live close to or away from your in-laws, one thing to remember is that you are happily married to your spouse now because your parents-in-law raised him with love and affection. The love of your life did not appear from nowhere; obviously, you didn't find him floating down a river one day or pick her from a tree like an apple. Your spouse is here today because your parents-in-law devoted twenty or thirty years of their lives to raising him.

Around 70 to 80 percent of the physical and inner characteristics that define who your spouse is today are inherited from your parents-in-law. So disliking your in-laws means that you dislike 70 to 80 percent of your spouse. Understanding this correlation will help you realize that you are contradicting yourself by loving your spouse but disliking your in-laws.

Your In-Law Is a Reflection of Your Future Self

Another piece of advice I would like to offer to those of you who cannot bear your nagging and controlling mother-in-law is to remember that you may one day become a parent-in-law yourself. Now that you know the pain of having to deal with difficult in-laws, you can safeguard against eventually causing similar pain to your son- or daughter-in-law by maintaining a humble attitude.

This may be an issue specific to my native country, Japan, but it seems that women are increasingly reluctant to marry because of the fear or the pain of having to deal with in-laws. I often hear that many people make it a condition of marriage that they will not be held responsible for taking care of their spouse's aged parents. But this same condition can work against you when you find yourself on the other side. You may be young now, but in forty or fifty years, you will be the same age as the mother- or father-in-law you so despise. It may seem a long way off now, but

sooner or later the time will come when you have to face the same situation from the opposite side.

The son or daughter that you have brought up and nurtured with all your love and care for twenty years will one day come to you with the person they want to marry. And you will not only have to welcome someone you barely know—someone you may not know any better than a stranger you walk past on the street—but may also have to bear the pain of being treated as a nuisance, perhaps in the same way that you treat your parents-in-law right now. What's more, they may tell you that they would like to live far away from you so that they don't have to take care of you.

As a parent, you may find this impermissible. You may tell them that you will not approve of their marriage. You may say that you can only approve of a marriage to someone you know very well and cannot and will not consent to your child marrying someone you barely know. You may tell them that you will never allow their marriage and that nothing will change your mind.

But of course you're destined to lose; you're powerless before a young couple with a bright future ahead of them. They will tell you that they don't need your permission to leave home, get married, and start a new family. By then, you might have forgotten that when you were younger, you felt the same way that this young couple feels; you may lament the misfortune of having such an ungrateful and naïve child and find yourself cursing them for the rest of your life.

We human beings have a tendency to see things only from our limited, self-centered perspective. And when the situation changes after a few decades, we often forget how we felt before. We forget that we used to feel exactly the same as our children do now and remember only that we have spent our whole life looking after our children and making sure they have clothing, food, housing, and education.

> We human beings have a tendency to see things only from our limited, self-centered perspective.

We may feel that our children should naturally want to give back

to us for all we've done and should start by marrying someone we like. But if we ever feel this way, the lesson we need to learn is that human beings tend to think in a selfish way and are apt to see things from a self-centered point of view.

We May Switch Relationship Roles in the Next Life

The second piece of wisdom I would like to share is to learn from your in-laws, because they have more life experience than you do. Most of us get a job and learn from our supervisors the life lessons required to be a successful member of society. But if you get married without going through this social training, you may need to learn these lessons from your in-laws. Your mother-in-law might simply be trying to give you a tough-love lesson so that you can survive in a tough world.

> All our life experiences are precious opportunities for our souls to grow.

Just as we cannot easily quit our job solely because we have a nasty boss, we cannot divorce just because our in-laws are hard on us. All our life experiences are precious opportunities for our souls to grow, and when we see our life from this perspective, we can be thankful for everyone we encounter, including our mean in-laws.

The last piece of wisdom I would like to share with you to help you improve your relationship with your in-laws is based on a spiritual truth. In most cases, we chose our marriage partner before we were born, which means that we most likely also chose our parents-in-law or at least knew who they would be. And between mothers-in-law and daughters-in-law in particular, relationship tension seems to be more or less a universal issue because they often share a deep spiritual bond. In many cases, their spiritual connection is much stronger than their spiritual tie with their own parents.

If we have a difficult relationship with our in-laws, we may find that our roles are reversed

in the next life. For example, you may be a daughter-in-law of your husband's mother now, but you may switch roles with her and become her mother-in-law the next time you are born into this world. How would you treat your mother-in-law if she were to become your daughter-in-law? Do you think you would be able to gladly approve of her as a wife for your son? Pondering this possibility will probably allow you to see the situation differently and find a way to improve your relationship with your in-laws.

3

"My Children Are Not Doing Well in School"

Parents Are a Child's Biggest Influence

Children's poor performance at school is a very common issue that parents run into. I presume that about as many as 99 percent of parents have had dealt with this problem at some point. And of those 99 percent, I would say that about 70 to 80 percent are dealing with issues relating to their child's academic achievements, while the remaining 20 to 30 percent are facing other issues, such as physical performance, behavior, and attitude.

In about 80 percent of cases, the parents of children with poor academic achievement did not do well in school themselves. Despite this, these parents tend to have high expectations for their children and demand that their children do much better. The children can most likely tell that their parents did not study hard when they were young and feel that their parents are making unreasonable demands. It is only natural that the children should want to rebel against their parents if they feel that they are imposing unfair demands.

> Children should want to rebel against their parents if they feel that their parents are imposing unfair demands.

In cases like this, instead of telling our children to study harder, we should take advantage of their rebellious attitude and tell them that we want them to experience the same types of hardships that we went through for not studying hard enough, so that they can learn their lesson the hard way. This approach will motivate our children to study harder.

So if you feel distressed by your children's poor performance at school, take a moment to examine your own academic capabilities. Did you have an excellent record at school? Are your expectations for your children too high compared to how you did at school? Remember, to produce splendid crops, we need to plant good seeds in good soil.

Children with Successful Parents Suffer Strong Pressure

What if both parents had a terrific academic record and are successful in their careers but still find their children not doing well in school? This could be a sign of an even more serious problem lurking beneath the surface.

Children of intelligent and capable parents constantly feel intimidated. To achieve excellence in their careers, their parents must have sacrificed and led a stoic lifestyle. And their bottled up frustration often distorts their personalities leading them to suppress their children. As a result, such children may constantly feel suffocated around their parents.

Some children whose parents hold respected positions in society become delinquent. Those born to parents who work in a profession of high moral standards, such as teachers, police officers, doctors,

or priests, for example, often rebel against their parents and get in trouble. This is because the children have to shoulder the load of the distortion created by the parents' pent-up stress.

> Children of highly capable parents engage in misconduct from their sense of guilt and to free themselves from their parents' repression.

A child whose father is the head of the PTA may see behind the scenes of the admirable gentleman; at home, he may be a sloppy, middle-aged man who constantly picks fights with his wife. Unable to bear this contradiction, the child may try to remove the veil of family secrecy by becoming a juvenile delinquent, in which case the child is acting as an angel in disguise.

Another case in which children of highly capable parents can fall behind and become delinquent is when their parents force strong feelings of guilt upon them. For example, children raised by a conservative Christian priest who preaches every day that people are sinners and must repent may feel that their freedom of the soul is suppressed, making them want to revolt. These children engage in misconduct such as shoplifting or bullying in an effort to escape from their sense of guilt and to free themselves from their parents' repression. Their delinquent behaviors are simply expressions of their inner pain. Their misconduct is often a sign that they are struggling to escape from the oppression and pressure that their soul suffers as a result of their parents' imposing their values upon their children.

A Self-Help Spirit Is the Best Education

One important perspective that we must remember as parents is that although we may have given birth to our children and share a close physical resemblance, our children have unique souls of their own that are both different and independent from us.

In the cycle of rebirth, we often end up reversing roles with the people we're close to. For example, in many cases, parents were their children's children in a previous life, or the children could have been the parents' mentors in a previous life. As we raise our children, we should keep in mind that our children could have been our parents or teachers in a past life and that we may have been given a chance to play the role of their parents in this lifetime to further our spiritual growth.

The most essential element in raising a child is cultivating a spirit of self-help. Education is not about producing our clones; our children do not have to act or think exactly the same way we teach them to. On the contrary, perhaps the best education we can offer at home is to raise our children so that they can live without our help and guide them

to become self-reliant, indepen-dent, and enterprising individuals.

> Our children have unique souls of their own that are both different and independent from us.

Of course, children can't be independent of their parents while they are still young. A certain degree of parental intervention is necessary while children are underage. But as they grow up and become more spiritually aware, parents need to gradually nurture a spirit of independence in their children. It is parents' job to make sure that their children become independent around the time they turn eighteen. This self-reliant spirit will allow our children to stand on their own two feet, lead others, and achieve great successes in life.

Whether or not we as parents are capable and successful in what we do, we should focus on how we can cultivate our children's unique strengths and consider how we can help them succeed in the future.

Some of us may be bothered if our children lag behind other children. But we should tell ourselves to maintain an attitude of "letting others mind their own business, and us our own."

We never know what life may bring. Someone with perfect physical health may enlist in the army, become a pilot, and then be shot down and die in a war, whereas someone who is in frail health may avoid fighting in the war and live to old age. Some fail in business because they are too smart, while others who were never considered "bright kids" achieve success through persis-tent hard work.

We won't know what will truly serve us until the very end of our life. So the important lesson we should teach our children is that they can open up a path in life regardless of the physical appear-ance or abilities they were born with and no matter what kind of environment they find themselves in. Many children today have grown up in a better environment than their parents did, which should work to their advantage. As their parents, we should encourage them to work hard to achieve their dreams by making use of all the privileges granted to them today.

4

"I'm Tired of Looking After My Sick Family Member"

Homemakers Are the Doctors and Nurses of Home Life

There must be thousands or even millions of people who are facing the difficult challenge of having to take care of their sick family members at home. This is an experience that no one can avoid; at least one of our family members falls ill at some point in the lives of each of us. But the fact that having to care for the sick is common doesn't make it any easier.

It is hard enough having a family member hospitalized, and it gets even tougher if we have to nurse the patient at home. If you are a full-time homemaker, you need to spend extra time attending to the family member in addition to your usual household chores. If you work outside

the home, you may not be able to look after the person at all.

Taking care of the sick is a lot of work, especially if you have to take care of an elderly parent with dementia who is confined to bed. This heavy burden will anguish your soul. You may feel completely helpless and complain, "How can I take control of my own life and build a new future when I'm forced to spend all my time taking care of my demented parent?"

What kind of attitude or mindset should we have if we find ourselves in this situation? Should we take it as an inescapable fate, or should we see it as an issue that we can solve through our own effort? Or should we send the

sick person to an institution?

Before you answer these questions, take a moment to consider this spiritual truth: the souls of the sick remain intact. We all had perfectly healthy and joyful lives when we were souls in the spirit world. But when we are born into this world and live in the flesh, we cannot avoid injury and sickness, because the physical body is imperfect.

> We all had perfectly healthy and joyful lives when we were souls in the spirit world.

One day, we may have to face a harsh reality of life: we may be in good health now, but we never know what might happen to us or to our loved ones down the line. So we should do what we can to prevent illness; we should manage our health by eating well and getting enough sleep and exercise.

It is part of the homemaker's job to provide nutritious care to make sure that the family members maintain good health. In other words, medical care is part of homemaking, and the homemaker is expected to perform the roles of doctor, nurse, and dietitian. In fact, those who can fulfill the role of the doctor, nurse, dietitian, and cook, as well as educator of children, should be highly valued.

Traditionally, women have been thought to be better fitted than men for homemaking because they have been thought to be tidier, more caring, and better with children. Particularly in older generations, men have sometimes not had much training in household chores and so have not been able to handle them as quickly and efficiently as women have. Of course, some women find themselves unfit for housework and childrearing, and some men are extremely good homemakers, but they are often treated as exceptions because women have generally been considered naturally adept at taking care of others, and men have often been pressured to take care of their families solely by earning money. As a result, many women have found a calling in fulfilling the role of doctor or nurse and have made it part of their mission to give love in these ways—by doing the work of angels.

Providing care for the family member who falls ill is part of homemaking. Homemakers may sometimes wonder why they have to go through such hardship, but homemaking is a professional job, like a doctor or nurse, that entails providing medical care in the home. Doctors would not be doing their job at all if they refused to treat their patients. Nurses would not be able to keep their job if they are reluctant to dressing a wound. Providing these kinds of care is all part of the homemaker's job. This is true even though homemakers are unpaid and are typically on call twenty-four hours a day.

Just as companies have articles of incorporation that state the purpose of the business, housework also has its own purpose as a professional job. Its scope of work and responsibilities include raising a family, maintaining family members' health, and providing nutritious meals, and in some situations, homemakers need to take on the role of doctor or nurse to provide the family members with the healthcare that they need. Thus, taking care of the sick at home is an integral and valuable part of the homemaker's job.

Help the Elderly Find a Purpose in Life

Even if you accept your responsibilities as a healthcare provider at home, you may still feel desperate when you think about the long and difficult years of looking after an elderly parent with dementia. But have you ever thought about what causes dementia? In many cases, those who develop dementia lack a sense of purpose in life. This tells us that we always need something to live for, even when we get old. As we get older, we increasingly feel vulnerable, and we begin to fear not being wanted

or needed. So the last thing we want to do when we take care of the elderly is treat them as a nuisance and take away their joy of living.

> We always need something to live for, even when we get old.

So, one kind of preventive care we can provide for the elderly is helping them find something to

live for. We can offer them tasks or a job in the home that they can find joy and meaning in. In this way, they can take part in a variety of activities and stay healthy even as they become older. If we help them build self-esteem, they will be able to live with a sense of fulfillment.

Sometimes, people develop dementia as a reaction to the unfavorable treatment they receive at home. If they are treated as a nuisance and cast off as if they were already dead, the only way they can resist is by developing a disease.

Treating old people as if they are a nuisance will only increase their risk of developing dementia. If you are the one who will most likely have to look after them, then it will serve you best to treat your parents and in-laws well to increase the chances that they will live long, healthy, and happy lives. Treasuring our elderly family members and helping them find a purpose in life is another crucial part of family life.

If you have bedridden family members who show no sign of recovery, perhaps the only thing you can do is pray: pray for their swift recovery, or if that's not possible, pray for their smooth return to heaven by the grace of God. Finally, you can also help yourself by preventing yourself from facing the same fate in your old age.

5

"I Can't Find the Right Person to Marry"

Finding a Spouse Is Like Finding a Job

I'm sure many women are seeking their ideal match and are wondering if they will ever find one. In fact, this is one of the major issues that women find quite distressing. But it seems to me that many of them actually behave in a way that prevents them from getting married. At the conscious level, they think they are seeking happiness, but they are in fact behaving in a way that attracts unhappiness. These people cling to their past failures forever and embrace them as if they are sitting on an egg of unhappiness, waiting for it to hatch into a huge disaster.

Those who firmly believe that they are destined to meet the ideal partner may wait for that fateful encounter forever and end up missing the opportunity to marry. But this may also mean that they are being too choosy about whom to marry. My advice to these women is to think of finding a spouse like choosing a career.

When we look for a job, we have to meet certain conditions that the company requires for the position, such as experience, education, physical fitness, or language skills. No one gets job offers from all the companies in the world; no matter how gifted you are, some companies will not find you suitable. Like everything else, employment is a match between supply and demand, and whether or not you are aware of it, there is always someone who wants to hire you.

For example, both age and educational background can be important factors in finding work. College graduates are older and more experienced than

high school graduates, and some people take a gap year between high school and college, which may or may not work to their advantage.

If a company is looking for high school graduates, even a diploma from the most prestigious university won't get you the job. You may find this unreasonable and try to persuade them that your college degree makes you the ideal candidate for the job. But the company will have its own reasons for preferring a high school graduate. Perhaps it has a policy of only hiring high school graduates to maintain harmonious relationships among coworkers. Or perhaps it simply does not have any open positions that require the skills of college graduates. So there is no point in getting exasperated about it.

We cannot always get the job we want or get into our first-choice company. We usually have to decide which job to take within a limited amount of time, so we have to settle for whichever company gives us the best offer.

Think of marriage as a limited-time opportunity. You might miss a chance to marry if you take as much time as you want. Just as you do when you are searching for a job, consider your competence, background, and the best timing

for you to get married. And if you realize that you need to make a decision within a year, accept the best opportunity you come across during this period.

> Consider your competence, background, and the best timing for you to get married.

One thing you need to be careful about is not to set your sights too high. Think of your future husband as the one doing the hiring, the one who will give you a sense of well-being for the rest of your life, and accept the opportunity within a given time period.

If you are rejected by your first choice, don't despair. Simply think of it as one of the many job interviews a job seeker typically goes to. We all get turned down in the course of job hunting. No matter how exceptional or talented we are, if we apply for jobs at ten companies, chances are that some of them will reject us. Rejection is simply a part of job hunting.

If your boyfriend tells you that he isn't planning on marrying you or your girlfriend refuses your marriage proposal, tell yourself that the company who interviewed you was not right for you. Don't let it bother you; instead, get moving to find another partner. One company's rejection in no way means that you are useless or no good. Moping around a pond despondently or sitting by a river feeling depressed will not help.

Simply tell yourself that just as you have expectations for your partner, others have their own needs, too, and that you'll find your match when both parties meet each other's needs.

So my advice is to set a fixed time limit for finding marriage opportunities and choose the best one from those available to you.

Find Contentment with Your Partner

Women who do not get married despite intending to tend to be indecisive; they often have a weak will, which makes them incapable of making decisions. On top of that, these people are often fastidious and set their sights very high. This tendency makes it even more difficult for them to make up their minds, and they keep missing their chance to get married and end up staying single their entire life.

Of course, you don't have to force yourself to marry someone that you instinctively dislike or someone you just cannot stand. But if you meet someone who may not be quite everything you were looking for in a spouse, or feel that you may not necessarily be destined to be together, but you find the person acceptable,

then I suggest that you consider marrying him.

Take courage and know that you'll be able to handle anything life may throw at you.

And don't spend too much time thinking about it. Be quick in your decision, and do it before you start pondering whether it's worth it, finding faults in your partner, or setting conditions for marriage. Take courage and know that you'll be able to handle anything life may throw at you. I'm sure your partner will feel glad to marry someone who's so decisive.

If you are still not sure about it, remember the job-hunting

scenario again. Let's say that one company offers you a job. If you tell them that you would like to accept it only if other companies reject you, that will only offend the company that offered you a job. If you go back to them three days later and tell them that you would like to accept their offer because you were turned down by your first- and second-choice companies, chances are that they will no longer want to hire you.

So, make a swift and bold decision when you receive a "job offer" from a "company," even if it is not your dream job. Try not to overestimate yourself, and be content with what you are offered. As the saying goes, when you try to grasp all, you will lose all.

Marry for Your Own Happiness, Not for the People Around You

If your circumstances make it difficult for you to find a spouse—for example, perhaps you are an only child who has to look after your aging parents or has to take over a failing family business—you are in a disadvantageous position. Instead of trying to find your ideal partner, you can increase your chances of finding a spouse by feeling grateful for any offer that may come to you.

The most important factor in determining your marriage partner is whether the two of you will be able to live happily together. As long as you agree on this point, you should compromise on other, secondary issues, such as whether to live close to or away from your parents.

> The most important factor in determining your marriage partner is whether the two of you will be able to live happily together.

If you prioritize the secondary issues—for example, what your parents say about the marriage or where you want to live—it may take forever to get married. So if you believe that you and your partner can create a happy life together, your best bet is to disregard what other people say and go ahead with the marriage.

"I Don't Know How to Deal with a Combative Family Member"

Forcing Our Values on Our Children Leads to Rebellion

Many families are suffering from conflict or violence. In my country Japan, teenagers turning violent against their parents is probably the most common problem. While we also have spouse-abuse issues, the majority of violent behavior at home is committed by adolescents and young adults. This has become a serious social issue in present-day Japan.

What triggers their aggressive behavior at home, and what are the effective solutions to these problems? One of the main causes is definitely stress.

The exam-based education system in Japan does not take into consideration students' non-academic strengths and interests.

Children's achievements are usually uniformly assessed based on rigid educational guidelines, and they are not allowed much freedom to pursue their interests outside of their studies. So children with unique talents sometimes rebel out of frustration with their failure to meet the school's standards.

In many cases, children react aggressively toward their parents when the parents force their own values on them. For example, parents may tell their children to behave or not to behave in certain ways in their personal affairs, studies, and career. This creates parent-child conflict that often results in more serious fights.

Some parents may tell their child, for instance, "You are going to be a doctor when you grow up, so you must study hard and go to medical school. And since we can not afford the tuition, you must study even harder to receive a scholarship." The child may study hard to fulfill his parents' wish but be unable to bear the constant pressure, and one day, his built-up stress may explode into violence.

In cases like this, we often find the root cause in the way the parents think. They probably believe that what they are doing is in their child's best interest. Perhaps the parents don't want their child to suffer the same setbacks or failures that prevented them from achieving their dreams. They may believe that they simply want to help their child become successful and are setting high standards out of parental love. But in the end, they are simply imposing their ideals on their child, which, in many cases, are not what the child wants at all.

What many parents don't realize is that their children do not necessarily think or feel the same way as they do. Although many parents believe that they know exactly what's on their children's minds, they usually have no idea what their teenage children are thinking about.

> What many parents don't realize is that their children do not necessarily think or feel the same way as they do.

The parents may be too busy with their own work to know what their children talk about with their friends or what their aspirations are, or they may simply not be able to gain sufficient information to know what is going on with their children. The children may value things that their parents would never expect.

Parents Should Trust Their Children and Lead by Example

Giving space to children so that they can pursue their own goals is one way to solve the problem of family conflict. Children rebel when their parents forget their own faults and scold their children for not meeting their expectations. So parents should reflect on themselves sincerely and ask themselves whether they are really living in a way that others can look up to. Children learn best by example, not by being told what to do or chastised for their shortcomings.

If children see their parents studying hard, they will eventually follow their example and start studying hard themselves. But children will not listen to the father who comes home drunk every night and spends every weekend on the golf course and then lectures them every time he sees them, "You have to study hard; otherwise you will end up like me." Similarly, it's only natural for children to start doing bad things if their mother is never home because she's busying herself with leisure activities.

The first thing the parents of delinquent children should do is to straighten themselves out and make an effort to create a good home. Next, they should acknowledge their children as unique individuals, stop meddling in their business too much, and give them room to go their own way.

> As long as there is a trust relationship between parents and children, the children will sooner or later learn to restrain themselves and start following the rules.

What's most important is that parents always trust their children. As long as there is a trust relationship between parents and children, the children will sooner or later learn to restrain themselves and start following the rules. Children often start behaving themselves when their parents compliment them on how good they are, because these positive words help them gain self-esteem. Conversely, distrusting children

and telling them how bad they are only makes them want to take revenge by getting into more trouble.

Strictly monitoring your children's behavior—for example, clandestinely reading their diary—is a sign of distrust that often triggers problems. Parents should also not make their children lose face. If, for example, you answer a phone call from your son's girlfriend and hang up, telling her that he is too busy with his studies to talk to her, it is only natural that he will be furious. He might tell you that he is serious about her and that he is even thinking of marrying her in the future. And if you tell him off, saying that he is still way too young to talk about marriage, the quarrel could easily escalate to physical violence. Similarly, you may worry if your young daughter starts getting calls from a boy and going out with him. You may be tempted to ground her or come up with reasons to keep her at home. But this will only make your daughter rebel.

We should always trust our children and make sure they feel trusted by telling them that we believe in them. Trust your daughter when you find out that she is going on a date with a young man. If you scold her for her behavior and try to stop her, her heart will only drift farther from you.

> We should always trust our children and make sure they feel trusted by telling them that we believe in them.

Some children turn rebellious against their parents because of excessive stress for failing to meet their parents' demands for academic achievement. If, after years of hard study, your son doesn't get into his first-choice college, he may feel like a complete failure. Constantly reminding him of his failure by criticizing him for not making it or telling him that you did better in school will only make him feel even more miserable and hopeless, and he will rebel as a matter of course. In a case like this, perseverance is the best policy for both parents and children: believe that, in the long run, difficult times will become the seeds of future success.

Create a Comfortable and Relaxing Home for Your Husband

Conflict between spouses is another common problem in the home. What can we do to solve this issue besides seeking professional help? One way is to search for the underlying reason for the conflict or aggressive behavior. If, for example, your spouse gets drunk every night and becomes argumentative, what do you think is making him or her do that? If you have ruled out alcoholism and other addiction problems, consider whether there is anything you might be able to do to improve the situation. What would an ideal partner do to help? Do you think your spouse might change his or her behavior if you did things differently on your end? Whenever we experience conflict in our relationships, it's always good to consider whether we ourselves might be doing something to contribute to the conflict.

Some people become argumentative or violent when they come under constant criticism at home. Suppose a wife, who is not so perfect herself, nags her husband about not getting ahead in a company when his coworkers have all been promoted, or about not having enough savings because his salary is so low. She might also complain that he is not spending enough time with the family or that they haven't had sex for the longest time. No one likes being blamed this way, and if a husband doesn't know what else to do, he might resort to going out and drinking himself into a stupor. Seeing him come home all drunk, the wife might further condemn her husband, which might only make things worse.

> The first thing you can do is stop criticizing your spouse and think about what you can do to change yourself.

So if you are struggling with conflict between you and your spouse, the first thing you can do is stop criticizing your spouse and think about what you can do to change yourself. You can improve the situation by trying to do what

you can to create a home where both you and your spouse can feel comfortable.

Another simple but effective solution is to prepare or bring home a good meal. A surprising number of men are epicures and enjoy fine food and drink. For these people, eating a delicious meal at home may ease their frustration.

Of course, there are other ways to please a spouse. Some people may be good-looking enough to delight their spouse's eye. But if we aren't looking like a movie star that day, preparing a tasty meal can be just as effective at helping our spouse relax. Sometimes it only takes small efforts like this to change the situation completely. Your spouse may simply be having a hard time at work, and a good meal may be all you need to help him or her feel better.

As a starter, why not try to prepare or bring home a delicious meal for your spouse every night? You might be pleasantly surprised by the positive changes you see in the home.

PART IV

The Unhappiness Syndrome at Work

**7 HABITS AND PRESCRIPTIONS FOR
SURVIVING THE BUSINESS WORLD**

1

"I'm Always Busy and Have No Time"

Our Work Lives Are a Daily Race against Time

The first thought pattern that we want to cure in this chapter is the feeling of never having enough time. This is an issue that many people in the business world struggle with. The majority of them, especially corporate employees, probably find themselves racing against time every day.

Some people spend one and a half hours commuting to work, which means that they spend three hours a day just for traveling to and from the office. If they start working at 9:00 a.m. and want to arrive at the office before their supervisor arrives, they have to be there half an hour earlier, by 8:30 a.m. To make it on time, they have to leave their home at 7:00 am, which means they have

to get up some time between 6:00 and 6:30 a.m. People in the competitive business world may work until around 7:00 p.m., or even work overtime until 9:00 p.m. And they don't always go straight home—they often grab something to eat or go out for a drink, so by the time they head home, it could well be 11:00 p.m., and they don't get home until after midnight, around 1:00 a.m.

Under the bright neon signs in the city, even midnight does not seem that late, but for someone staying at home, it is the dead of night. Family members may be waiting, furious at how late the worker is coming home. If they grab something quick to eat and take a shower, it's almost 2:00

a.m. by the time they go to sleep. Since they have to get up at 6:00 the next morning, they get less than five hours of sleep. Even without the commute and socializing, some people work late into the night and come home as late as 3:00 a.m.

> The majority of corporate employees probably find themselves racing against time every day.

Even on the weekends, workers often can't use all their time for themselves. Some people have to work—those in sales, for example, may have to entertain clients or schedule meetings on the weekend. Some end up spending every Saturday on a golf course with their clients. And even if they get Sundays off, they need to spend some time with their family. This means that they do not even have a single day in a week to rest and unwind. Indeed, the life of a corporate worker can be very tough.

I've experienced this type of lifestyle myself. When I used to work for a trading company, I remember feeling so exhausted on Saturday that sometimes I slept through the day and didn't wake up until evening. I was so completely overcome by fatigue that I had to catch up on my sleep on Saturdays; otherwise I wasn't confident that I could make it through the rest of the week. I'm sure a lot of people store up on their sleep on weekends.

A good many people who lead this kind of lifestyle are probably tired of it and are eagerly counting the days until their retirement twenty years later. They may dream of the day when they can take a nap whenever they want to, enjoy gardening, and lounge around the house all day long.

Live True to Yourself

Since you'll spend most of your waking hours working, managing your time or using your time effectively all comes down to whether, in light of your plans for the future, you consider your current job worth dedicating your whole life to. If you find purpose

and meaning in what you do and feel that your current job is your calling in which you can achieve your lifelong dream, then you will be able to keep at it even if it means struggling for promotion through managerial and executive positions until you finally get to the top. But not many people can maintain such enthusiasm and motivation throughout their career.

According to research, more than 80 percent of the newly employed expect to reach a managerial position, and nearly half aim to hold a top executive position. But in a follow-up survey five years later, the same people estimated their chances of promotion to be much lower than they had anticipated. Their expectations decreased again after ten years, and finally, fifteen years after the initial survey, most of them had given up on promotion altogether. By then, they felt lucky if they were assigned an

assistant. They no longer desired any title and only wished to stay in their current position until retirement.

> Ask yourself what your heart's desire is and what it means for you to live true to yourself.

Ponder how much purpose and meaning you find in your current job. If your dream is to become a manager or executive at your current company, it may be important for you to devote yourself fully to your job. First and foremost, ask yourself what your heart's desire is and what it means for you to live true to yourself. Your answer will help you determine how you should use each of the twenty-four hours in your day and how you want to spend each day of your week.

Work More Efficiently and Spend Less Time Socializing

The best way to make time is to improve your work efficiency as much as possible so as to cut

down on the amount of time you spend on your job. Focus on your main tasks and finish them

quickly, while at the same time achieving desired results. Make it a rule to finish your work within your regular working hours and not work overtime. This is how we can get sufficient sleep and make free time for things outside of work.

About 80 percent of the time, we work overtime merely out of habit. We need to be aware of this and give serious thought to how we can work faster. We should make a plan to finish our work on time and do all we can to carry that plan out.

Building competence will definitely speed up our work. If we can finish by 3:00 p.m. what might take another person until 8:00 p.m., we gain five hours to work on something else until we leave for the day. We might use the time to work on a difficult task or start a new project while our coworkers are finishing up their day's work.

Another way to save time is to let go of the idea that you can make up for your inability by working overtime or socializing with coworkers on weekends. Those who are not confident of their competence often try to compensate by working late into the night, socializing with their coworkers, or playing golf with

their clients. But these tactics alone won't help you get ahead in the business world. Being sociable can be a plus factor, but not a deciding factor. Especially in the current, difficult economic climate, employees are evaluated based on their capabilities and achievements.

> Being a skilled and accomplished worker is what will earn you success in the corporate world.

It's naïve to think that your social skills alone will earn you a high position if you lack the skills to get work done. Of course, you will be highly valued if you are very competent and at the same time are good with people, but if you have to choose between the two, develop your work skills over your socializing skills. Being a skilled and accomplished worker is what will earn you success in the corporate world.

So the first key to getting more time for ourselves is to work more efficiently, and the second key is to stop depending on your social skills outside the office, whether that means drinking with

coworkers at night or entertaining your clients on weekends. Instead, gain recognition for your performance and achievements. Meanwhile, do your best to build a good relationship with your colleagues during regular office hours. These are the two essential keys to creating time in the busyness of day-to-day life.

Make Use of the Time You Have Created

Once you have successfully made time for yourself, how should you use it? Of course, you have to spend a certain amount of time on social obligations, but try to limit them to no more than 20 percent of your total free time. For example, you may need to use one weekday evening each week for socializing, but use the remaining four for your own sake.

How you will use these four evenings depends on your perspective on life and your vision for the future. If you would like to enrich your life, you could spend them trying out a wide range of activities. If, on the other hand, you have a goal you wish to achieve outside of your work, then you can use the time to continue your studies in the fields that interest you.

Lack of sleep is one of the main issues that many business people face, so if you want to make more time for yourself, I suggest staying away from the temptation of alcohol. So as not to appear rude or impersonal, you may want to go out with your colleagues several times a year, but otherwise, staying out of regular drinking outings will probably serve you best.

> Create time for yourself
> little by little,
> and use that time to
> build a firm foundation
> for your personal life.

If work is all you've got, you may experience a severe sense of loss when you retire. To prevent this, create time for yourself little by little, and use that time to build a firm foundation for your personal life. This philosophy will become increasingly important for today's and tomorrow's corporate employees.

2

"I'm Not Good at Doing Business"

Think about What You Will Say Beforehand

Many people in business feel distressed by their inability to make business deals. Even those who graduated from school with honors sometimes find themselves not getting ahead in their company, and in most cases, this is due to poor negotiating skills.

What are the characteristics of those who are not good at negotiating? Some people get very nervous when they have to talk in front of others; they go completely blank and lose themselves. Some simply do not like debating or using bargaining tactics. These people are not competitive by nature and would much rather seek peace of mind. This type of person would probably be more suited for monkhood, but unfortunately, they have become sales representatives who wear suits and sit at negotiation tables.

> As long as you know what you will say, having a talk with others should not be too difficult.

For these people, I would like to offer three pieces of advice. First, do your homework, and think about what you will say before the meeting. A lot of people feel pressured when they think they have to come up with something to say on the spot. Picture a scenario of what your client may say. List the things you will say to make a convincing argument, and memorize your list. As long as you know what you will say, having a talk with others should not be too difficult.

So the first thing you can do if you fret about negotiations or debates is think about what you will say beforehand and practice it well in advance.

Change How You Talk Accordingly

My second piece of advice to those who fear business negotiations is to change how you talk depending on who you are talking to. Those who fear negotiating probably have experienced failures in the past that still haunt them; they may have killed a business deal, have their offer turned down, or failed in their sales pitch in a fierce competition against a rival company. We humans have a tendency to develop a fearful, negative attitude toward challenges that we have proactively taken on but failed in. Those who have tried to negotiate and failed often lose confidence in their ability.

So, how can we gain confidence in our negotiating ability? The most important point is to know the person we are talking to—how he or she thinks, feels, and behaves. If we become caught up with what we have to say, we make the mistake of overlooking their reactions. I have seen people who are so immersed in what they are saying that they don't notice their clients' signs of discomfort, such as yawning, fidgeting, and playing with their pen. These people are unlikely to clinch top deals. Memorizing a sales pitch and using it every time without taking into account who the clients are or what they are looking for will only lead to rejection and failure.

> Understanding different types of people will help us learn to talk in ways that are appropriate for each person.

What we need to do is to learn how to change the way we talk and what we say according to the person we are talking to. And to do this, we need to deepen our understanding of people by studying various types of people. Every time we enter into negotiations, we should carefully watch our negotiating partner, as if we are conducting research on human beings. Through careful observation, we can learn how this type of person thinks, talks, and responds. Understanding different types of people will help us learn to talk in ways that are appropriate for each person.

We can hardly ever proceed with negotiations in the way we want to, so we need to change our negotiating tactics according to our clients. Negotiation is a process of meeting both parties' wants and needs, so we should be able to think as our client thinks. In this respect, memorizing what we have said can be effective; by remembering what worked for which kinds of people, we can increase our chances of success with future clients.

Solve Your Personal Problems First

The third piece of advice I would like to offer is to solve your personal problems. Those who find themselves unsuccessful in negotiations often have outstanding issues in their private life. We may find the root of our problem in the least expected area. When we have family issues, such as a difficult relationship with a spouse that leads to daily fighting, a family member struggling with illness, or a grown child who doesn't go to school or get a job, this distress becomes part of our aura, preventing us from becoming persistent negotiators.

Although our public life is separate from our private life, serious problems in our private life can have an impact on our public life, so spotting and solving our private problems in their early stages is crucial to our success at work. It is very unlikely that we'll be able to fully devote ourselves to our work if we have domestic conflicts at home. These issues can affect our work.

> Spotting and solving our private problems in their early stages is crucial to our success at work.

Although it may seem to be taking the long way, we should solve our private problems first, before trying to devote ourselves to work. Otherwise, we will be caught in a dilemma between personal issues and work issues and end up not being able to solve any of them.

If you are having an issue with your spouse, make sure you do your family duties on the weekends and, if necessary, go home early every night to do whatever it takes to solve the problem.

Another underlying cause of negotiating failure could be a painful memory of a divorce or a feeling of despair about the prospect of remaining single your entire life. People with these experiences often develop a fear of the opposite sex and lose confidence in themselves. As a result, they often find it difficult to devote themselves to their work, and that can have a negative impact on their bargaining power.

If you have trouble getting over a divorce, search for a new partner. If you have difficulty finding a partner, you may have set your sights too high, so consider settling for someone available. If you don't think you can find anyone, you can seek help from a match maker. You can also ask your parents, coworkers, or friends for their opinions. When you don't know what to do, it is sometimes better to leave the matter in someone else's hands. If your family and friends disagree over which person you should choose, then follow the advice of the person you respect most or the person who is on the same wavelength as you.

I hope that these three pieces of advice will help you improve your negotiation skills. Gaining bargaining power is about cultivating your strength as a human being; it's about building self-confidence and persistence. An ability to negotiate will open a way forward for you. Conversely, a lack of bargaining power often leads to a negative assessment of our entire character as a person, so it is all the more important to develop this capability.

The first step for those who fear negotiations is to heal and rebuild themselves so they can gain self-confidence and start living with unflagging vitality. Strengthen your inner self, use all your brain power, and boldly start negotiating your business deals. This is how you can open up a new path.

3

"I Don't Get Along with My Boss"

A Good Relationship with Your Supervisor Is Essential to Your Career Success

I believe that over 90 percent of company workers have some kind of workplace relationship problem. The thing is, we don't usually get to choose the person we work for, and a lot of times, we don't even get to choose who works under us. So to create a good working environment, we have to learn to straighten out tangled relationships.

Of course, we can be lucky or unlucky when it comes to the people we work with. If we have a good manager, we can devote ourselves to our work and make use of our strengths, but if we do not get along with our manager, it will make things difficult for us at work. This is an issue that

everyone in the business world will probably have to deal with sooner or later.

As a basic rule, we will not be able to succeed unless we are on good terms with our direct supervisor. Even if we somehow manage to pave a road to success, it will not lead to great success.

So what should we do when we don't get along with the person we work for? In many ways, the structure of corporate life creates a culture like that of a feudal society. Employees are expected to devote themselves to serving the company and contributing to its growth, and to get ahead, they have to be liked by "the nobles"— the company's higher-ups,

managers, and chief officers. This is something we simply have to accept.

Occasionally, people manage to become successful in their company even though they have a difficult relationship with their immediate supervisor. Someone else who is in an even higher position may give them a chance to get ahead. But in many cases, these people will have made enemies somewhere along the line and will eventually be cast aside.

Excessive self-confidence is often the reason that many of these people do not get along with their supervisors. When they don't agree with the way things are done, they go about their work even if it does not accord with what their supervisor wants. They may think that they have done a good job, but they end up receiving a low performance review. This kind of experience is frustrating, and the worker may be tempted to request to work under someone else or to move to a different department. But this is a common pitfall that many people fall into in the corporate world.

If you have a difficult relationship with your manager or supervisor, the first thing to know is

that your assertiveness may be part of the problem. Recognizing each employee's opinion is not necessarily the company's first priority. A company's main goal is to survive and develop as an organization, and your ego may not have a place in this project.

> Excessive self-confidence is often the reason that many of these people do not get along with their supervisors.

How do you feel about the fact your company's management has placed above you the supervisor that you criticize as inept? No matter what your position is, someone among the higher-ups is probably responsible for evaluating your supervisor's performance.

Suppose your supervisor is in a managerial position. Her performance should be assessed by the general manager or an executive officer. So the fact that she is placed above you means that the management trusts her, that she does a good job, and that they recognize her competency. If she

is as incompetent as you believe she is, she will not retain her position for long. In that case, it's simply a matter of time, and all you have to do is be patient and wait for her to leave.

But either way, the top management must have had a reason for assigning her to her current position. You may not understand or agree with their decision, but your disagreement may also mean that you are unlikely to join the ranks of that company's top management. If you are planning to stay in your current company, my advice is to refrain from voicing strong criticism of your supervisor.

Respect People in Higher Positions

Another common characteristic we can find in those who often invite conflict with others is a tendency to be judgmental. So if you find yourself constantly in a difficult relationship, look within and ponder whether you have a hidden desire to crush those in power.

People with a Robin Hood spirit who wish to crush the strong to protect the weak may become popular with those who work under them but may intimidate those who work above them. Conversely, people who are unpopular among their colleagues may be very highly valued by those in higher positions.

Which of these types of people do you think will move up the ladder of success? Although it may seem unfair, it is the latter group.

This is because those in higher positions have authority over personnel issues. Winning popularity among our superiors can help us advance in our career, even if we are disliked by those who work under us.

Perhaps in the world of gangsters, things might be different, and winning popularity among our subordinates would help us get more important positions within the gang. But most business organizations have a rigid and organized structure, and the upper management has final say in personnel decisions. So to get ahead in the organization, it's absolutely essential that management evaluates us highly.

Another challenge is that we don't always know why we became

popular among our colleagues and subordinates in the first place. We might have won their hearts by taking them out to eat and inviting them to our homes, but they might not be able to accurately assess our competence at work or know how our superiors are evaluating our decisions.

> Often a desire to crush the strong arises out of an inferiority complex.

If you are popular among those who work under you but those above you have a low opinion of you, it means either that you are misunderstanding something or that you have a chivalrous sense of justice that makes you want to bring down the powerful and save the weak. But often a desire to crush the strong arises out of an inferiority complex. Such people often have a pain in their souls that makes them feel threatened by people who have power over others; they feel as though they need to fight back to guard against further damage. This aversion may have its roots in a setback or failure they suffered in the past; the memory of that failure then comes back to haunt them whenever they see people in positions of power. But holding on to this sentiment won't help us grow; nor will it help us advance in our career.

We humans need to find purpose and set goals in life. To improve ourselves, we should respect those who are more capable and more experienced than we are. If we seek career success, we should refrain from criticizing those above us, because our success depends on the success of those we work for.

Give Others Credit for the Work You've Done

People in positions of power struggle to find competent employees. They need a good team of people working under them to get the best results. With capable people, success comes easily, even without any effort on their part.

In other words, the surest path to career advancement is

helping your supervisor move up the career ladder, no matter what type of person he or she is. We should make it our goal to help our direct supervisor get promoted and work with strong determination and enthusiasm to achieve that goal. This is how we get into the fast track of career success in the corporate world. So put aside any personal likes or dislikes, and do all you can to help your supervisor succeed.

> The surest path to career advancement is helping your supervisor move up the career ladder.

When you do things for others like this, remember not to take credit for them. If you go around bragging that it was your idea or that you did all the work, someone may trip you up.

Though it may sound paradoxical, if you want to get promoted, give others the credit for the work you've done. Those who feel that they are not properly recognized for the work they do may want to take all the credit for their achievements. But giving others credit instead will certainly open up a path to success. If you do your job to the very best of your ability and then give the credit to your superior, you will surely climb the ladder of success.

4

"I Don't Know How to Handle a Demotion"

Perseverance Is the Key

It hurts to get demoted or assigned an obviously unimportant job. And if you are a corporate employee, this is something that you can't do anything about.

But why and when do we get demoted? There are two main reasons for demotion. First, we may have failed in our work or at least failed to achieve the expected results. Second, we may have conflicts in relationships with our coworkers.

How should we take our demotion if it's the result of our own failure? If we fail in our work, we should not gloss over it but instead admit that we made a mistake while keeping a positive attitude. We may lose our title or have our pay cut because of our failure, but the last thing we should do is to put the blame on others or external circumstances. We should accept responsibility for our mistake and prepare to persevere through a difficult next six months or year.

While I sympathize with those who have been the targets of restructuring, that is sometimes what a company has to do to survive in the very competitive business world. Big corporations evaluate people based on their efficiency and capability, so those who are not competent can easily get demoted or assigned a minor post. In fact, many of the large trading companies in Japan have subsidiaries as places to send off those who get demoted. Japanese trading companies have as many as one to two hundred affiliate companies, and the majority of them are there to accommodate

the deadwood. They do this to keep the company's atmosphere vibrant and energetic.

> You can open a new path when you accept the situation quietly and continue to work steadily and calmly.

In the international trading company I used to work for, I saw a lot of people relegated to minor posts and shunted off their career track. I would often come in one day to find an assistant promoted to a manager and a manager demoted to an assistant. The assistant that you oversaw yesterday would suddenly become your new boss who would now be evaluating your work. It may sound very cruel, and it was certainly tough on the person who was demoted, but this kind of thing happens all the time in the business world. If you find yourself in this situation, criticizing others will do you no good. You can open a new path when you accept the situation quietly and continue to

work steadily and calmly. Instead of being discouraged, keep working diligently and build up skills outside of work until you get your next chance.

We all make mistakes, and they are often accidental rather than intentional. The people around us may see our failure as an unfortunate accident. Even if it was an accident, though, we should not think of it simply as something that we weren't able to do anything about. Whatever others may say, we should keep working hard to gain another chance and persevere until a new opportunity comes our way.

Especially when we are relegated to a minor post, we should grit our teeth and persevere for at least a year. This may be the toughest time of our life, but that's why we cannot give up. If we hang on for one more year while doing what we can, someone will surely come to open a path for us. Even if we are written off as no good, we should keep up our efforts; others will be surprised by our mettle and realize that we have potential after all.

Reflect on the Thoughts and Actions that Led to the Failure

Some people are demoted not because they made a big mistake, but because they didn't get along with their coworkers.

Many of the people who have difficulty getting ahead at work despite their capability and talent are what I call "the scholar type." They are extremely smart, but they prefer to work alone. They don't like to work as a team, and they are usually not suited for communicating and negotiating with others. In many cases, they are assigned to work on a very specific task.

In Japanese banks, for example, there is a position known as the research officer, which is filled by middle-age and elderly people. Some of the people who are assigned to this position are considered to have no prospects of promotion. The same is true of many posts that have the prefix "vice" or "deputy." In Japanese trading companies, if you see people whose titles have one of those prefixes, it often means that they have been sidetracked from the main career track. Although their titles may make them look important, they usually don't have actual work to do.

These people often end up in these positions because they had strained relationships with their colleagues in previous posts. The root cause of their difficult work relationships lies in their childhood and has to do with how they built their character. We don't develop our personality overnight; tendencies and habits that we acquire beginning in childhood eventually become who we are.

> Self-reflection is the starting point for discovering why you've had interpersonal conflicts.

If you were demoted because of a difficult relationship at work, try reflecting on yourself. Self-reflection is the starting point for discovering why you've had interpersonal conflicts.

Look deep within and contemplate these questions: "Is there anything inauthentic about the

way I act, think, or feel? What is distinctive about my character? Did my behavior or action make others uncomfortable? How do I differ from people who are good at building harmonious relationships with others?"

Take about thirty minutes every day and reflect back on yourself at different stages of your life:

1. Zero to three years old
2. Four to six years old
3. First to third grade
4. Fourth to sixth grade
5. Seventh to ninth grade
6. Tenth to twelfth grade
7. College years
8. Your first job
9. And so on, up until you reach the present day.

As you review your thoughts and actions in each phase, see how your present self has developed, and try to find the root cause of the problems you've had.

You may discover that your childhood waywardness is the root cause of your current problems with others. Perhaps being an only child made it difficult for you to learn how to build relationships. Or maybe you grew up in the country and are having a tough time adjusting to the fast pace of city life. Or you may realize that you chose a career that doesn't suit your character.

When you thoroughly review and ponder your life history this way, you will no doubt discover the cause of your present struggles. Regardless of what path you take in your career, you can always learn from your mistakes, correct your path in life, and improve yourself as a person.

Turn Demotion into an Opportunity for Improvement

Those who are demoted or assigned a dead-end job will find that their work is undemanding and gives them a lot of free time. Some people may find nothing to do and end up spending all day reading the newspaper. This may sound depressing, but if we look at it from a different perspective, they also have the advantage of being able to go home early. No one is going to complain if they

leave the office at five o'clock sharp every evening. No one will criticize them if they spend extra time relaxing at home.

> Demotion or relegation can turn out to be the best time for personal growth.

So, if you ever find yourself in this situation, use it as an opportunity to recharge. You may miss your busy work life at first, but you might as well enjoy a slower-paced life and having free time on your hands. Use this period to look within and reflect on yourself. If you can use this time to refine your character, you may find a chance to rebound from your adversity. We all experience slumps in life, but these are the times for recharging, rebuilding, and improving ourselves to become better people altogether.

We need to be able to sense and catch the ebb and flow of life. When we are riding a wave of success, we should work as hard as we can, and when the wave subsides, we should take time to recharge, accumulate knowledge, and improve ourselves.

In a sense, demotion or relegation can turn out to be the best time for personal growth. If we just change our perspective, we will see that it's actually our greatest opportunity to achieve self-realization. Working on the front line usually doesn't give us any free time, so we often lose sight of ourselves. But when we are demoted or assigned a minor position, we get all the time we need to prepare ourselves to take the next step in our career. We should appreciate and rejoice in this precious time as a gift from heaven and transform it into a seed of greater success.

5

"I Don't Know If I Should Change Jobs"

If You Are Not Confident about Leaving, Stay in Your Current Job

Whether or not your current job is the right one for you is another common question. Those who are currently looking for a job may not be sure where to look. The problem is often that we don't know what the right job for us is and whether our current job is our calling.

I myself faced this issue when I was struggling to decide when to quit my previous job and devote myself wholly to the path of the Truths, so I know how hard it is to make a decision to change careers.

I think that most people have difficulty with this because they are not sure what criteria to base their decision on. Desperately wanting to know the answer, they

may seek advice from their friends and counselors. Some may even visit a fortune-teller or psychic, only to find themselves in further confusion.

My advice to these people is quite simple: if you cannot make up your mind, stay in your current job. If you feel lost about what to do, it often means that it's not your heart's desire to change jobs and that there is still a chance that you'll have a change of heart after you quit your current job.

I recommend that you hang on in your current job for six months to a year while you develop your abilities. This will enable you to gain new knowledge or skills that you can use either in your current job or in your new job, should

you ultimately decide to move on. These new abilities may also help you become a more versatile person with the skills to work in a variety of fields.

You will know in your heart when the time is right. You will feel a strong urge to leave your present job and find a new job, or something will happen that will force you to quit your current job whether you like it or not. Your manager may become an angel in disguise and create a situation that forces you to leave. The nasty coworker you despise so much might actually help you decide to move on, so you should be grateful for him. Or your family may put you in a position that will give you no option but to quit your present job. Whatever it is, something will happen to drive you into a career change.

Look within and see if you find a strong desire to change jobs, or look around and see if you find yourself in a situation that forces you to make that choice.

So to decide whether you should change jobs, look within and see if you find a strong desire to do so, or look around and see if you find yourself in a situation that forces you to make that choice.

And once you have made up your mind, don't waste another minute. Take action to embark on your new career. Although it's best to stay put while we are still undecided, once you've made your decision, you should not doubt it even for a second; take courage and determinedly move forward on the new path you have chosen.

Avoid being too optimistic about your new career. There's no dream job that will give us everything we've ever wanted and bring us lasting happiness. We should be determined to do whatever it takes to be successful, no matter what circumstances we find ourselves in. It is this strong self-help spirit that will open up a path to success in our new career.

We should not base our decision only on an expectation of good things to come, such as a salary increase. Instead, we need to consider whether our determination is strong enough to carve out a new path in a new career.

Three Qualities of Successful New Business Owners

Among the people considering leaving their current job, some may be planning on starting their own business. Out of the many who dream of one day leaving their job to become independent, only about 20 percent succeed. The odds are that one in five will be better off, another one will have about the same level of income, and the remaining three in five will have less income than before.

> It takes a big commitment, strong determination, and tremendous vitality to succeed on our own.

Starting our own business may sound like a dream come true, but in reality, it takes a big commitment, strong determination, and tremendous vitality to succeed on our own. Many corporate workers mistakenly think that they owe their achievements to their ability alone when they owe a great deal to the company they work for. So it is often hard to tell how much they will be able to do when they strike out on their own. If we wish to test our own abilities by becoming independent, we have to be determined to do it all on our own, without expecting backing from anyone else.

The most essential element for successfully starting a business is an independent spirit. Having the strong mettle to pull off the difficult task of starting and running a business all on your own, without assistance or help from others, is the first condition for becoming a successful new business owner.

The second essential quality is a keen sense of money. A simple way to tell if you will be able to succeed at starting up your own company is to look at the amount of money you have saved during the years that you were employed. If you haven't managed to save as much as your colleagues in similar positions have on average, then you are less likely to be successful on your own, because it probably means that you are a spendthrift, which is a tendency that prevents people

from becoming successful new business owners.

Many owners of start-up businesses fail because they lack a keen sense of money. Knowing the value of money and accumulating enough capital to invest in a new venture on our own are basic elements of success in a start-up business. We should become independent only when we have accumulated enough capital to invest in the new venture on our own. The corporate mentality—an assumption of strong backing from our company—leads to failure when we become the sole proprietor of our own business.

Saving money is about balancing expenditures against income, and this is an indispensable ability for a business owner. People who are loose with money tend to be optimistic about their success; they often think that luck will help them make a name for themselves, or they hope that an opportunity will turn up somehow to bring them success. But this way of thinking will only bring them failure as a business owner, so they would be better off staying with the company they work for. The ability to make ends meet and minimize risks while considering future prospects is another basic and integral quality of a successful business owner.

The third quality of a successful new business owner is an attractive personality. If your decision to leave was based on your unpopularity at work, chances are that you will not be successful in your new venture either.

People don't work just for money; they work because they want to. People naturally want to help those who are good-natured; conversely, people don't want to help those they despise. So being a likable person is essential if you are going to start a business on your own. You also need to have an air of success if you want to become successful.

So if you would like to start your own business, reflect on yourself by asking the following questions:

1. Do I have the "self-help spirit"? Am I determined to succeed through my own efforts?
2. Have I been able to save money? Do I have a keen sense of money?
3. Do I have a good personality that attracts others? Am I the type of person that people would support and help in an emergency?

If your answers to all these questions are "yes," you have a good chance of becoming one in five people who will be successful in their start-up business. But if you answered "no" to two or three of them, it means that you are better off working for someone else, so I recommend that you either keep your present job or look for a job in another company.

6

"I'm Struggling Financially"

Do You Feel Guilty about Earning Money?

Money-related problems, such as debt and poverty, have brought pain and suffering to many people throughout the ages. There are two main causes of money problems. The first is reckless spending habits. Some people get carried away when money comes in, and they splurge on all kinds of things. A classic example is squandering your income on gambling, including horse racing, lottery tickets, and going to casinos. A variation of this is indulging in wildcat speculation on the stock market. These people lose money and end up suffering from debt and poverty simply because they don't know how to use money wisely.

The second cause is a lack of sufficient income. People with this problem lead meager lives and don't seem to get anywhere.

They settle for their current job or standard of living because they have low self-esteem. They often limit their potential by telling themselves that they are no good and that they can never improve their life. They've already given up on themselves and have no ambition or willingness to try anything new. These people have been working in the same old rut for many years but haven't been able to save any money to treat themselves to any luxuries. They have become used to living hand-to-mouth and even develop a fear of earning more than they do now. This is a typical symptom of the unhappiness syndrome. Deep down, they are scared of becoming rich, so they unconsciously develop a habit of keeping money out of their life.

This habit arises out of a sense of guilt about money. People who feel this way are often devout believers. Those who have studied religious teachings, whether from Christianity, Buddhism, or other religions, tend to develop a strong belief that greed is a sin and money is evil. That's why, often unconsciously, they use up the money that comes in, choose a job that will make it hard to earn good money, or botch up right when they hear that they are getting a raise, so as to prevent more money from coming in.

These religious souls have a subconscious desire for suffering: a lust for martyrdom, a longing to carry their cross, and a wish to be crucified. They find meaning in their misfortunes and so treasure debt and poverty as trials that they need to fight and overcome.

> Self-sacrificial souls don't feel contented when their life is smooth sailing.

These self-sacrificial souls, no matter what age they are born in, don't feel contented when their life is smooth sailing. As soon as a great opportunity for success presents itself, they begin to fear that something equally unfortunate will befall them. So they can never get out of a life of poverty.

Embrace Wealth and Set a Noble Goal

I would like to offer three pieces of advice for people with money problems. My first piece of advice is to be prudent with spending. To accumulate wealth, we must lead a frugal life and save money. The golden rule is never to spend more than we earn and to save part of our income. By gradually increasing our savings every month, we can taste the fruits of wealth. A frugal lifestyle is the first step out of a life of poverty.

My second suggestion is to try out new things to improve your work. As you work every day, continue searching for a better way of doing things. Make new discoveries, and make every effort to cultivate your talent. This will help increase your pay.

My third piece of advice is to overcome a negative mentality. Let go of your subconscious desire for poverty and suffering, which is driving you into debt. Take to heart the message that becoming rich is not a sin and luxury isn't your enemy.

Some people feel exasperated when they see others enjoying a lavish lifestyle, accusing them of being "bourgeois." But it truly is a worthwhile endeavor to use our financial wealth to contribute to society by helping many people live better lives.

> It is economic wealth that will give us the power to improve the world.

If we are suffering from poverty, how can we make the world a better place? Blaming the world will not get us anywhere. It is economic wealth that will give us the power to improve the world; the wealthy will have much more influence over the world than the deprived.

What matters most is the goal you wish to achieve in life. If you truly wish to live a life of misery and suffering because you think that this will bring you peace of mind, then you may have no choice but to live that way. But if your goal is to become a leader who can guide many people to happiness, then you need to immediately discard your tendency to embrace poverty and shift your focus to taking on bigger tasks.

A poverty mentality often manifests itself in real life. Even if we live frugally, we may one day squander all the money we've saved unless we let go of this subconscious wish to stay poor. If you feel that you have this tendency, I suggest that you thoroughly reflect on your thoughts and feelings deep down inside.

7

"My Business Is on the Verge of Bankruptcy"

Hard Times Test Our Ingenuity

Whether a company is large or small, bankruptcy is a serious issue for the business owners. Each company's situation may be different. One business owner may know that his company will go bankrupt within two months, while another may have to close his business when the next check bounces. Yet another may be struggling to pay back debt and may not know how long her business will last.

What triggers bankruptcy may also vary. It could be flagging sales, and the owner may not even know why sales have gone down. Providing good products and being honest may not be good enough, since some companies make profits by unscrupulous means. Some companies are forced to go under because their competitor has taken over the market.

Each business owner has his or her story. A mom-and-pop grocery store that has been in the family for generations may have lost its customers to a supermarket that has opened nearby. The parents can no longer afford to send their children to college, and there is a good chance that the family will have to close the store soon. Or the owner of a steel manufacturing company may have seen sales plunge due to a recession. He sees no way out of his predicament and despairs of his future.

Needless to say, the economic climate does affect business performance. Businesses that have done well for years in a booming economy may suddenly find their

sales slump and verge on bank-ruptcy as soon as they are hit by recession. But at the same time, some companies continue to grow even during a recession. So perhaps we should think of economic recession as a time when our ingenuity is tested.

When business conditions are good, it seems as if anyone can run a successful business. That's why many people start a new business—they're trying to taste the fruits of success. But this creates competition, and as a result, struggling companies are forced to go out of business.

No one plans to go bankrupt when they start a business. And it is extremely hard to accept a business failure. But however cruel it may seem, this is the way of the world. When there is an excess of supply, some businesses will have to leave and find a new field elsewhere. What matters most is which group you will belong to. Will you be able to persevere and survive and be chosen by the goddess of fortune,

or will you be deemed unnecessary and abandoned by her?

If we want to survive in our current industry, we need to come up with innovative ideas. We have to think of or do something that none of our competitors does; we have to create something new and unique to stand out from other companies. Another way to save our company from bankruptcy may be to diversify our business.

> Think calmly and
> search for a way to
> bring innovation to
> your business.

Our management capability is tested not when we increase our sales in a booming economy, but when we manage to survive a recession with a solid business base. So if your company is on the brink of bankruptcy, please think calmly and search for a way to bring innovation to your business.

Consider Going into a Different Field

If, in the end, you couldn't survive the competition, no matter what

you did or how much you tried, simply accept it as your fate. In

Mother Nature, for both plants and animals, natural selection occurs when the population of any one species increases beyond a certain limit. Competition occurs and reduces the size of that species until it goes back to a certain level. This is a law of nature.

This same law is at work in human society to an extent. Life would be difficult if everyone had the same occupation. Imagine a world where everyone you meet is a doctor, half the population are police officers, or fish markets are the only place to buy food. For society to function, we need all kinds of occupations, including butchers, farmers, and fishers. Even if you want to start a fish market, if there are already a lot of fish markets in your area, you'd be better off opening a grocery or hardware store. Society adjusts itself to maintain a balance among a variety of professions.

So if you look at your current circumstances and feel that you are the one who's likely to be weeded out, I suggest that you strive to find a new job or new field that will suit you. Sometimes, we just have to accept our fate; stubbornly fighting against it won't get us anywhere.

> If you are good at one job, you will most likely be successful in other businesses, too.

You may not want to change your occupation because it's been your family business for generations, or perhaps simply because you love the job. But these things shouldn't limit your potential. If you are good at one job, you will most likely be successful in other businesses, too. So be open to other options.

Let Go of Your Pride and Be Pragmatic

The key to good management is the ability to balance revenue against expenditure. The reason a company is now facing bankruptcy is quite simple: it's earning less than it's spending.

To reduce deficits, we need to balance our revenues and expen-

ditures. In other words, we need to either increase our income or reduce our costs. If, after careful consideration, you see no prospect of increasing sales in your current business, your only other option is to cut down on expenses, and the first item to work on is your fixed expenditures. You also need to consider how you can reduce unnecessary purchases and an undue amount of stock.

Sometimes our vanity gets in our way of cutting costs. For example, do you want to make yourself look good by renting a big office in a high-rise building in a prime location? Do you have a lot of unnecessary desks when there's practically no one to use them? Do you give your staff large bonuses when you can't even pay your bills? Do you always purchase your supplies from the same wholesaler without checking for competitive quotes or negotiating a better price? Balancing revenue and expenditures by either increasing earnings or reducing expenses is the only way to avoid bankruptcy. So be innovative, make new discoveries, and invent new products and services to increase the company's revenue. Or reduce overall expenses by

cutting down on fixed costs, such as the office rent or property lease.

> Balancing revenue and expenditures is the only way to avoid bankruptcy.

Our ego may tell us to keep expanding our business and never retreat. But we have to be prepared to retreat when necessary; otherwise we will lose everything. A good example of this is how the Japanese fought in World War II: the Japanese army had no hope of victory but kept on fighting, choosing an honorable death rather than surrender. Remember, we always have an option to retreat. We need to pull back when necessary, and sometimes we must pull back altogether.

If you find yourself on the verge of bankruptcy, face the reality squarely and examine yourself honestly to see if you are driven by pride. If you think you are, then let go of your pride and consider what you need to do from a pragmatic perspective. I'm sure you will come up with new ideas to help you move forward.

PART V

The Unhappiness Syndrome in Spiritual Life

4 HABITS AND PRESCRIPTIONS FOR OVERCOMING DOUBT AND FEAR

1

"I'm Scared of Death"

Rest Assured that the Afterworld Does Exist

I estimate that more than 90 percent of people fear death. And about half would probably say that they don't believe in life after death while thinking, "But what if?" in the back of their mind. Even these people cannot deny the afterlife completely.

So many people are afraid of dying because they are uncertain about life after death. Although we hear a lot of stories about the world after death, we can't tell whether they're authentic, because those who have traveled to the other world almost never come back to this world. And it's only natural for people to fear the unknown.

We are not afraid of visiting foreign countries, because we hear about what they are like from people who have been

there. If people who went abroad disappeared and never came back, we would be too frightened to even think about going abroad ourselves.

> We continue to exist even after we die and lose our physical bodies.

On top of that, we mostly learn about the world after death from spooky or horror stories about the dead and ghosts. So what we are afraid of is not death itself but ghosts. When many people think of the afterworld, they imagine turning into a ghost, and it is this idea that terrifies them, leading them to deny the existence of such a horrifying place.

But what kind of world really awaits us after death? Before answering this question, there is one truth that we all need to know: we continue to exist even after we die and lose our physical bodies. I have experienced this world firsthand, and I am 100 percent sure of its existence. That's why I have published numerous books about the truth of the spirit world's existence and what that world is really like.

A Good Map of the Afterworld Will Eliminate the Fear of Death

Although hell does exist, heaven is truly a world of bliss inhabited by numerous wonderful spirits. Knowing that this magnificent world exists will give people great hope.

If it is fear of the unknown that makes us afraid of death, a clear map of the afterworld should eliminate our fear. We would definitely feel uneasy if we had to visit a foreign country without any information about our destination. But we would feel more comfortable and secure about our trip if we had the proper maps and guidebooks.

I'm sure you'd be anxious if you had to go to a remote jungle in a foreign country without a map or travel guide. But you would probably feel more relaxed if you had a visitor's guide that told you what to expect when you got there. Similarly, we develop fear of death because, to many of us, the afterworld is like a dense jungle in a remote island, a place where many people get lost and never come back.

But even if we go to a bookstore to find a guidebook about the spirit world, most of the ones we find are creepy stories of how vengeful spirits and ghosts haunt humans and bring pain and suffering. Many psychics try to awe people by telling horror stories about hell. These kinds of information can be effective to a certain extent in sharing the truth about the spirit world. But they should be also sharing the wonderful aspects of the spirit world.

> Those who live honestly and with a pure heart should find an equally good and bright world in which to live after death.

When you look at the people living in this world on earth, how do they appear to you? If you see a den of iniquity, you may also see pandemonium unfolding before your eyes in the world after death. But it's unlikely that you only see evil in this world. And it's probably hard to believe that all these good people would go to the horrifying world of hell. It's only fair that those who live honestly and with a pure heart should find an equally good and bright world in which to live after death.

The world we refer to as "the other world" consists of multiple layers of realms stretching from the fourth to the ninth dimension, and this has been the subject of cutting-edge research in physics. Scientists have mathematically proven the existence of a multi-dimensional world—with the third dimension enveloped by the fourth dimension, the fourth by the fifth, and so on, all the way up to the ninth dimension—but they have yet to grasp what kinds of worlds these different dimensions actually are.

I have written numerous books that offer detailed descriptions of this multidimensional world that exists beyond this physical world. The most prominent ones are the trilogy *The Laws of the Sun*, *The Golden Laws*, and *The Laws of Eternity* (published under the title *The Nine Dimensions* in the United States). In particular, *The Laws of Eternity* offers a clear and thorough explanation about the structure of the other world.

Belief in the Afterlife Will Serve Us Well

People who fear death fall into two types. The first type includes people who fear dying because they don't believe in the existence of the other world and don't know what to expect when they die. The second type includes people who believe in the afterlife but are afraid that they may go to hell and fear what awaits them at their destination. People of the second type can prepare themselves by learning about the different worlds that exist in the afterworld. Knowledge of the spirit world will help them conquer their fear.

For the first type of people, those who doubt the existence of the afterworld or believe that they cease to exist at their death, I would like to pose the following question: "Which way of life do you think will make you happier at the end of your life: living with a belief that the other world exists or living with a belief that nothing exists after you die?"

Suppose you are now forty years old and have another thirty-five years left until you die. Is your idea of happiness living with a belief that no matter what you do during the next thirty-five years, you will be cremated and buried at the end, and all that will remain is a handful of bones and ashes?

If everything ended with death, it would mean that all the ethics, philosophies, and religions in this world are in vain. Why do you wish to improve your character? For what purpose do you study, work hard, and become friends with the people you meet in life? For what reason do you strive for a better life?

If our existence vanished at death, our life would be empty. There would be no point in making any effort or studying hard to improve ourselves. There would be no need to try to become a better person either. It would mean that we are all being tricked into doing all the things we are trying so hard to do. Sure, self-improvement may lead to higher status or income, which may give us temporary happiness, but if everything ends at death, these would indeed be empty pleasures.

Isn't it much better to believe that you have a unique individual soul that will continue to exist forever, even after you die? In that case, all the efforts we make in this world are worthwhile because we can take everything we have earned and learned with us to the other world when we die.

Isn't it much better to believe that you have a unique individual soul that will continue to exist forever, even after you die?

Which way of thinking do you think will lead you to true

happiness? Believing that everything will vanish when you die or believing that your soul will live on and your efforts in this world will help you live a wonderful life even after you die? Which of the two do you want to bet on? I have definitive proof that the other world does exist. So I can assure you that you will win a happy life if you bet on a belief in the afterlife.

Carefully consider which way of thinking will lead you to greater happiness. In the end, it will serve you to accept the truth and humbly learn about the other world. You will never have to fear death once you know about the afterworld and understand that how you live in this world will determine the kind of world you will go to after you die. The only people who need to fear death are vicious people who cause harm to others, show no repentance, and feel no remorse for their actions. If you don't become one of them but instead live in a way that you can truly be proud of, there is nothing for you to worry about.

2

"I Disagree with My Spouse's Religious Beliefs"

Faith Strengthens the Marriage Bond

What should we do when we disagree with our family member's religious beliefs? If the husband is a Buddhist while his wife is a Christian, their religious differences could lead to problems at home. Some couples marry knowing that they have different religious beliefs, but in some cases, one or both of them decides to join a new faith after they get married, which could give rise to conflicts between their beliefs. They would be preoccupied with trying to persuade one another to join their religion.

But before we go on, let us ponder on this question: Do a husband and wife need to share the same religious beliefs? I would say that a couple who shares the same faith can forge a very strong bond, which can be the basis of happiness.

In recent years, we have seen a massive increase in the divorce rate, which can often break a family apart. This phenomenon partly has to do with people's loss of faith in God. More and more people believe that marriage is like a legal agreement; they no longer believe that the grace of God has brought them together. As a result, they tend not to take marriage and divorce seriously.

> When we share the same faith, we can overcome any crisis by basing our decisions on our beliefs.

Another problem that many married couples have is a lack of conversation. This could be because of differences in their

lifestyles. If the wife chooses to become a full-time mom to focus on housework and child-rearing, she won't be able to take the time to study or gain new knowledge about the outside world. On the other hand, the husband may be involved with a variety of projects at work that require him to learn and be familiar with information such as the latest trends in the market and business conditions. The knowledge gap between the wife and husband may actually cause a lack of communication if it means that they run out of things to talk about.

Sharing the same faith helps in a situation like this. They can strengthen their bond by learning together and encouraging each other to study their religious teachings. We human beings need something to rely on. And when we share the same faith, we can overcome any crisis by basing our decisions on our beliefs. This is why I believe that it is best for a married couple to share the same religious beliefs.

Change Yourself If You Want to Win Over Your Spouse

Having said this, however, you should probably not try to force your partner to convert to your religion, because doing so can easily turn your home into a living hell.

Suppose a wife has found a new faith. Her husband may oppose her joining it, even if it is a wonderful religion. And he probably has his reasons, too. In fact, many people become very suspicious when it comes to joining a new religious group. They cannot believe in something without first seeing how it can benefit them.

If you really want to win over your spouse, what's important is not to force him to change his beliefs right away, but to change yourself first. You need to prove how wonderful your religion is by changing your mental attitude, improving your state of mind, and becoming a better person. If you continue to make improvements for two to three years, people around you will surely see the difference. Your colleagues and friends will notice the change in you, so there is no doubt that your spouse, who is the person closest to you, will see it too.

We are mistaken if we think

that simply registering our name or joining a religious group will save our souls. Some Christians say that belonging to their church is the only path to salvation. This may be one way of converting others, but I don't think that enrollment in a church automatically purifies or improves our souls. We should know better. Signing our name is only a beginning and nothing more. Even if the group offers wonderful teachings, membership alone will not bring salvation. Instead, we have to study the teachings diligently and strive to make them our own.

> Having a spouse of a different faith tests our religious tolerance.

So the first step to take is to change yourself. You need to prove to your partner how much your new religion has changed you. Show her what a wonderful person you have become. Keep trying until your spouse is so impressed with the improvements you have made that she is motivated to study it for herself.

To put it another way, we should never force our opinion on others or think that just because we believe in something, other people should too. In this respect, having a spouse of a different faith tests our religious tolerance.

Intolerance is one main reason people despise religion. Some people may believe that belonging to their specific denomination or learning their denomination's spiritual teachings is the only path to salvation. But this is a very worldly view of human beings. God and the divine spirits are generous and merciful. So we should try to find the positive aspects of the teachings of other religions, learn from them, and use them to improve our life. What we need now is religious tolerance and generosity of heart. This is a very basic and fundamental way of thinking about religion.

3

"I'm Disheartened by a Psychic Reading"

Diviners Tend to Give Pessimistic Predictions

Many people visit a psychic or fortune-teller to find out what will happen to them in the future or to find solutions for their problems. I presume that about 70 percent of people have experienced some sort of fortune-telling, if we include palm readings, tarot readings, and horoscopes. Even those who do not believe in the existence of the spirit world sometimes rely on divine power from the world beyond to discover what the future has in store for them, often out of thrilling curiosity or the hope of dispelling anxiety about the unknown future.

While the decision to consult a fortune-teller is entirely up to you, one thing you might want to keep in mind is that most psychics and fortune-tellers tend to predict misfortunes. I find this very disappointing, because when we hear that something bad will happen, we often fall victim to fear and feel threatened to do something to avoid it.

We all get sick and have relationship problems at some point in life, so predictions of illness and conflicts with others will most likely come true. The type of person who wants to have a reading done tends to be highly suggestible, and as a result they often end up fulfilling the ill-starred "fate" that the psychic has prophesied and giving their lives a turn for the worse. Some fortune-tellers seem to exaggerate their negative predictions to intimidate their clients, and that doesn't bring happiness to anyone. For this reason, I would like to ask those who make their living through divination to emphasize the positive and deemphasize the negative.

> We can also overcome the trials of life with the power of positive and bright thoughts.

We may try everything we can to avoid misfortune, but we can also overcome the trials of life with the power of positive and bright thoughts. So it is unfair to predict someone's bankruptcy, death, or other ill fortune when we have the power to practice positive thinking. No one has the right to say that we were born under an unlucky star, that we are ill-fated, or that our name, palm lines, and birthday forecast misfortune.

Diviners may believe that they are helping the people and contributing to the world. They may believe themselves to be living angels, but the fact is that many of them will not return to the world of angels after they die. Even the warm-hearted ones often go to the Sennin Realm in Minor Heaven*. And doomsayers who instill fear and dishearten many will find themselves doomed to hell. I find it ironic that the whole time they were predicting other people's futures, they weren't able to foresee their own future.

The only good thing about divination is that it acquaints people with the existence of the spirit world. Even those who do not believe in religion may develop some interest in palmistry, astrology, or onomancy. This can bring some people spiritual awakening, however faint it may be, and may become the key to the door of redemption should they find themselves in hell after death. Unbelief in the existence of the afterworld and the spirits often makes it extremely difficult for people to find salvation when they die. So offering a glimpse of the spirit world to nonbelievers can be considered the diviner's main achievement.

---

* The spirit world is made up of many different realms layered both horizontally and vertically. Minor Heaven exists at the back of heaven and consists of various realms inhabited by spirits who focus exclusively on exercising metaphysical forces. They do not value love or enlightenment and thus tend to lack human warmth and kindness. (Refer to *The Nine Dimensions*, IRH Press, 2012.)

Our Destiny Is Determined by Three Elements

When do we feel the need to consult a fortune-teller or psychic? In most cases, it is when we have specific issues on our mind. For example, we might be worried about marriage, divorce, exams, illness, or other incidents. When we feel distressed, it's natural to want to seek advice from someone with a higher awareness.

We all experience difficult times when our heart is torn apart and we can find no way out of a tangled situation. At such times, we look for someone we can lean on, someone who can offer solutions. But we can also look at life as a workbook of challenges to overcome. We are given a series of problems to solve in life, not a series of answers. This is because we are supposed to overcome the challenges on our own so that we can become stronger. So asking someone else to solve our own problems is not necessary good for us.

It is often said that each of us humans has a destiny to fulfill, but what exactly is destiny? While some aspects of our densities are fixed and unchangeable, there are other aspects that we can change. We can decide how much we want to take control of our destiny, and how much we can change the course of our life ultimately depends on our own will.

What are the elements that make up our destiny? The first element is the plan we made for ourselves before we were born into this world. The second is the amount of effort we make during our life on earth. And the third is the spiritual influences we receive from our guardian and guiding spirits and from negative spirits that try to harm us. Our fate is determined by the combination of these three elements.

> We can significantly change our fate during the course of our life on earth.

One thing I would like you to remember is that none of us, before we are born, creates a plan

to end up in hell. We may have thought of that possibility in the back of our mind as a worst-case scenario, but we all believe that it could never happen to us.

But the fact of the matter is that a considerable number of people do end up in hell, and this shows that we can significantly change our fate during the course of our life on earth. And how our fate changes depends on the second element, our effort, and the third element, our spiritual influences.

You will be fine as long as you lead a decent life under the guidance of your guardian spirit. But you may face the danger of taking the wrong path if you harbor negative thoughts that attract evil spirits. If you are possessed by negative spirits and live under their influence, your mind will be drawn to a lower and darker world.

Three Keys to Improving Our Destiny

Although we face the risk of falling into hell, we can also open the door to a new and better future by practicing the following three keys. The first key is to constantly look within your mind and correct any mistakes you find. If you find any wrong thoughts, ask for forgiveness and make amends immediately.

We humans cannot avoid making mistakes, but what's important is not avoiding them, but correcting the mistakes we make. We should not aim to become someone who never makes a mistake in life, but rather someone who can correct mistakes and turn them around to create something better out of them. This is how we can become truly great.

> Your destiny will take a better course when you embrace thoughts of love for others and wish to bring happiness to many people.

The second key is to resolve to love as many people as possible during the course of your life.

Your destiny will take a better course when you embrace thoughts of love for others and wish to bring happiness to many people. Those who don't have fate on their side are often only concerned about themselves. No matter how hard they try, they can't open the way forward or win others' support. This is because they are only thinking about what's good for them and lack love for others. A path will open before those who do their job with love for others. And those who help others without expecting anything in return will receive help from others when they face crises.

In the course of life, adversaries may appear and plunge us into confusion, but collaborators will also appear to help us out. When I look back over my life, I see that many people offered help when I least expected it. After all, human beings are not altogether bad. We may sometimes be misunderstood, but nevertheless, we should always have love for others and live for the sake of others.

The third key is to believe that human beings are essentially good. A forlorn belief that human nature is fundamentally evil will not help us create a wonderful world; it will lead instead to a miserable life. What is vital is to believe that all human beings, including ourselves and those around us, are fundamentally good. A jubilant belief in the goodness of human nature is essential to inviting good fortune into our lives and to creating an ideal world on earth.

No matter what kind of bleak future a fortune-teller predicts, we can always find a way to conquer any ill fortune as long as we constantly seek the right mind, have a heart filled with love, and believe in the goodness of human beings. When you live with this attitude and strive to improve yourself every day, you will find a path to a bright future opening before you. At that time, you will be able to prove the doomsayer wrong.

4

"I Don't Know How to Console the Souls of My Ancestors"

Our Ancestors Are Wishing for Our Happiness

Some religions stress the importance of consoling the spirits of the ancestors, and they often attribute family misfortunes such as illness, injury, and bankruptcy to the lost souls of the family's ancestors. In most cases, these religions say that the lost soul of an ancestor from more than four generations ago is causing the problem and that they need to hold memorial services for the ancestors to solve the problem. This is how some religious groups take advantage of people's misfortunes: they cash in on memorial services.

They blame an ancestor from more than four generation ago because it has to be a dead person who's causing whatever problem the family is struggling with. Grandparents and great-grandparents may still be fit and healthy, so they play it safe by naming an even older ancestor. These religious groups put all the blame on this ancestor and say that holding memorial services for the lost soul is the only way the family can solve the problem and live happily.

This is a catch-all technique. No matter what problems the family is struggling with, they can simply say that the lost soul of their ancestor is causing them. The family members have no way of verifying that it is really their fourth-generation ancestor that's causing the problem, or, for that matter, that it's a tenth- or twentieth-generation ancestor. For the religious practitioners,

this is simply an easy way to get business: as long as they place the blame on the ancestors, they can earn a fee for their service.

I was shocked to learn that this kind of "business" is popular throughout my native country, Japan. Of course, there are probably some cases where the souls of ancestors *are* lost, but even then, these ancestors would not intentionally harm their descendants.

> The best way to console their souls and help them find salvation is to let them know where they went wrong and guide them to the right path.

There is simply no reason why ancestors would wish to torment their own children, grandchildren, or great-grandchildren. The truth is that they are praying for their descendants' prosperity. Even if they themselves have fallen into hell, few of them would consciously want to harm their descendants. Some desperate, "drowned" souls may come to their descendants for help to "catch at a straw." Still, even in this situation, their intention is not to cause harm to their descendants.

These souls are seeking help because they do not know where they went wrong when they were alive. They don't understand why they made wrong decisions or why they are suffering now. So, the best way to console their souls and help them find salvation is to let them know where they went wrong and guide them to the right path. These souls are simply lost as to what to do because they find themselves in a world that they didn't expect to end up in, probably because they lived as they pleased while on earth. But, if by some turn of events, they curse their descendants for their own misfortunes, then they are committing another sin that will only increase their suffering.

Live in a Way that Will Help Your Ancestors

If we really wish for our ancestors to be happy in heaven and want to console their souls, we should send them prayers of gratitude. We should also lead the right way of life and live a life filled with light. This is how we can help the souls of deceased family members.

> Our ancestors will be able to happily rest in peace if they see their descendants flourishing and prospering.

If you are a parent, you wish for the happiness of your children more than anything. Even if you have to go to prison for your sins, you still want your children to be happy. Likewise, if you are a grandparent, you are happy to see your grandchildren's smiling faces. In the same way, our ancestors will be able to happily rest in peace if they see their descendants flourishing and prospering.

As their descendants, the first thing we should do is seek the right mind and create a wonderful, harmonious family so that we can show them what good thoughts and actions are. This will encourage our ancestors to reflect back on their own thoughts and deeds. Self-reflection is something we have to do on our own and by our own will. It is not something that others can force us to do. But we can help our ancestors reflect on their lives by showing them what it means to live in the right way.

We should also send thoughts of gratitude to our ancestors from time to time. We are here now because of our ancestors, and we are the fruits of our grandparents' and great-grandparents' love. Conversely, if you are praying for the salvation of your lost ancestors only because you believe that they are hampering your happiness, your prayers will not bring happiness to your ancestors or to yourself, no matter how hard you pray. Similarly, repeatedly reciting a sutra whose meaning you don't even understand will not help your ancestors enter heaven.

Another possible problem with holding a memorial service for our ancestors is that it can attract wandering spirits and other spirits with ties to that religion, instead of our own ancestors. If we

commemorate our ancestors at home every day, many wandering spirits and lost souls may come to our house, hoping that these prayer services will save their souls. As a result, we may end up inviting more troubles from these negative spirits.

To avoid this, we should first study the Truths thoroughly and practice them in our day-to-day lives. By living with a positive state of mind, we can sever our connections with evil spirits. The first step is to fill ourselves with light, because when our souls are shining brightly, evil spirits cannot come near us. Transforming ourselves this way is the path to true happiness.

Finally, for those who are interested, my organization, Happy Science, offers a memorial service ceremony for ancestors at both our head temples and our local temples. Our service can help you offer prayers and gratitude to your ancestors and other deceased family members safely and under the guidance of our ministers while receiving light from the divine spirits in heaven.*

---

* For more information about Happy Science's memorial services, please contact your nearest Happy Science temple.

afterword

In this book, I have listed common negative thought patterns that lead to unhappiness and offered solutions for each of them in the same way I would if I were answering personal letters.

I hope that I have successfully explained the true nature of the cancer called "unhappiness" and provided clear and effective cures for this syndrome.

Ryuho Okawa
Founder and CEO
Happy Science Group

ABOUT THE AUTHOR

RYUHO OKAWA is Global Visionary, a renowned spiritual leader, and international best-selling author with a simple goal: to help people find true happiness and create a better world.

His deep compassion and sense of responsibility for the happiness of each individual has prompted him to publish over 2,100 titles of religious, spiritual, and self-development teachings, covering a broad range of topics including how our thoughts influence reality, the nature of love, and the path to enlightenment. He also writes on the topics of management and economy, as well as the relationship between religion and politics in the global context. To date, Okawa's books have sold over 100 million copies worldwide and been translated into 28 languages.

Okawa has dedicated himself to improving society and creating a better world. In 1986, Okawa founded Happy Science as a spiritual movement dedicated to bringing greater happiness to humankind by uniting religions and cultures to live in harmony. Happy Science has grown rapidly from its beginnings in Japan to a worldwide organization with over twelve million members. Okawa is compassionately committed to the spiritual growth of others. In addition to writing and publishing books, he continues to give lectures around the world.

ABOUT HAPPY SCIENCE

Happy Science is a global movement that empowers individuals to find purpose and spiritual happiness and to share that happiness with their families, societies, and the world. With more than twelve million members around the world, Happy Science aims to increase awareness of spiritual truths and expand our capacity for love, compassion, and joy so that together we can create the kind of world we all wish to live in.

Activities at Happy Science are based on the Principles of Happiness (Love, Wisdom, Self-Reflection, and Progress). These principles embrace worldwide philosophies and beliefs, transcending boundaries of culture and religions.

Love teaches us to give ourselves freely without expecting anything in return; it encompasses giving, nurturing, and forgiveness.

Wisdom leads us to the insights of spiritual truths, and opens us to the true meaning of life and the will of God (the universe, the highest power, Buddha).

Self-Reflection brings a mindful, nonjudgmental lens to our thoughts and actions to help us find our truest selves—the essence of our souls—and deepen our connection to the highest power. It helps us attain a clean and peaceful mind and leads us to the right life path.

Progress emphasizes the positive, dynamic aspects of our spiritual growth—actions we can take to manifest and spread happiness around the world. It's a path that not only expands our soul growth, but also furthers the collective potential of the world we live in.

Programs and Events

The doors of Happy Science are open to all. We offer a variety of programs and events, including self-exploration and self-growth programs, spiritual seminars, meditation and contemplation sessions, study groups, and book events.

Our programs are designed to:

- Deepen your understanding of your purpose and meaning in life
- Improve your relationships and increase your capacity to love unconditionally
- Attain a peace of mind, decrease anxiety and stress, and feel positive
- Gain deeper insights and broader perspective on the world
- Learn how to overcome life's challenges
  . . . and much more.

For more information, visit happyscience-na.org or happy-science.org.

International Seminars

Each year, friends from all over the world join our international seminars, held at our faith centers in Japan. Different programs are offered each year and cover a wide variety of topics, including improving relationships, practicing the Eightfold Path to enlightenment, and loving yourself, to name just a few.

Happy Science Monthly

Our monthly publication covers the latest featured lectures, members' life-changing experiences and other news from members around the world, book reviews, and many other topics. Downloadable PDF files are available at happyscience-na.org. Copies and back issues in Portuguese, Chinese, and other languages are available upon request. For more information, contact us via e-mail at tokyo@happy-science.org.

CONTACT INFORMATION

Happy Science is a worldwide organization with faith centers around the globe. For a comprehensive list of centers, visit the worldwide directory at happy-science. org or happyscience-na.org. The following are some of the many Happy Science locations:

UNITED STATES AND CANADA

New York
79 Franklin Street
New York, NY 10013
Phone: 212-343-7972
Fax: 212-343-7973
Email: ny@happy-science.org
Website: newyork.happyscience-na.org

New Jersey
725 River Rd. #102B
Edgewater, NJ 07020
Phone: 201-313-0127
Fax: 201-313-0120
Email: nj@happy-science.org
Website: newjersey.happyscience-na.org

San Francisco
525 Clinton Street
Redwood City, CA 94062
Phone&Fax: 650-363-2777
Email: sf@happy-science.org
Website: sanfrancisco.happy
science-na.org

Atlanta
1874 Piedmont Ave.
NE Suite 360-C
Atlanta, GA 30324
Phone: 404-892-7770
Email: atlanta@happy-science.org
Website: atlanta.happyscience-na.org

Florida
5208 8th St. Zephyrhills, FL
33542
Phone: 813-715-0000
Fax: 813-715-0010
Email: florida@happy-science.org
Website: florida.happyscience-na.org

Los Angeles
1590 E. Del Mar Blvd.
Pasadena, CA 91106
Phone: 626-395-7775
Fax: 626-395-7776
Email: la@happy-science.org
Website: losangeles.happyscience-na.org

Orange County
10231 Slater Ave #204
Fountain Valley, CA 92708
Phone: 714-745-1140
Email: oc@happy-science.org

San Diego
Email: sandiego@happy-science.org

Hawaii
1221 Kapiolani Blvd. Suite 920
Honolulu, HI 96814
Phone: 808-591-9772
Fax: 808-591-9776
Email: hi@happy-science.org
Website: hawaii.happyscience-na.org

Kauai
4504 Kukui Street
Dragon Building Suite 21
Kapaa, HI 96746
Phone: 808-822-7007
Fax: 808-822-6007
Email: kauai-hi@happy-science.org
Website: kauai.happyscience-na.org

Toronto
323 College Street
Toronto, ON M5T 1S2 Canada
Phone&Fax: 1-416-901-3747
Email: toronto@happy-science.org
Website: happy-science.ca

Vancouver
#212-2609 East 49th Avenue
Vancouver, BC, V5S 1J9 Canada
Phone: 1-604-437-7735
Fax: 1-604-437-7764
Email: vancouver@happy-science.org
Website: happy-science.ca

INTERNATIONAL

Tokyo
1-6-7 Togoshi, Shinagawa
Tokyo, 142-0041 Japan
Phone: 81-3-6384-5770
Fax: 81-3-6384-5776
Email: tokyo@happy-science.org
Website: happy-science.org

London
3 Margaret Street
London, W1W 8RE
United Kingdom
Phone: 44-20-7323-9255
Fax: 44-20-7323-9344
Email: eu@happy-science.org
Website: happyscience-uk.org

Sydney

516 Pacific Hwy Lane Cove North,
NSW 2066 Australia
Phone: 61-2-9411-2877
Fax: 61-2-9411-2822
Email: sydney@happy-science.org

Brazil Headquarters

Rua. Domingos de Morais 1154,
Vila Mariana, Sao Paulo,
CEP 04009-002 Brazil
Phone: 55-11-5088-3800
Fax: 55-11-5088-3806
Email: sp@happy-science.org
Website: cienciadafelicidade.com.br

Jundiai

Rua Congo, 447, Jd. Bonfiglioli
Jundiai, CEP 13207-340
Phone: 55-11-4587-5952
Email: jundiai@happy-sciece.org

Seoul

74, Sadang-ro 27-gil, Dongjak-gu,
Seoul, Korea
Phone: 82-2-3478-8777
Fax: 82-2- 3478-9777
Email: korea@happy-science.org
Website: happyscience-korea.org

Taipei

No. 89, Lane 155, Dunhua N. Road
Songshan District, Taipei City 105
Taiwan
Phone: 886-2-2719-9377
Fax: 886-2-2719-5570
Email: taiwan@happy-science.org
Website: happyscience-tw.org

Malaysia

No 22A, Block2, Jalil Link, Jalan
Jalil Jaya 2, Bukit Jalil 57000
Kuala Lumpur Malaysia
Phone: 60-3-8998-7877
Fax: 60-3-8998-7977
Email: Malaysia@happy-science.org
Website: happyscience.org.my

Nepal

Kathmandu Metropolitan City
Ward No. 15, Ring Road,
Kimdol, Sitapaila
Kathmandu Nepal
Phone: 977-1-427-2931
Email: nepal@happy-science.org

Uganda

Plot 877 Rubaga Road, Kampala
P.O. Box 34130
Kampala, Uganda
Phone: 256-79-3238-002
Email: uganda@happy-science.org
Website: happyscience-uganda.org

ABOUT IRH PRESS USA INC.

IRH Press USA Inc. was founded in 2013 as an affiliated firm of IRH Press Co., Ltd. Based in New York, the press publishes books in various categories including spirituality, religion, and self-improvement and publishes books by Ryuho Okawa, the author of 100 million books sold worldwide. For more information, visit OkawaBooks.com.

Follow us on:
Facebook: MasterOkawaBooks
Twitter: OkawaBooks
Goodreads: RyuhoOkawa
Instagram: OkawaBooks
Pinterest: OkawaBooks

BOOKS BY RYUHO OKAWA

Invitation to Happiness
7 Inspirations from Your Inner Angel

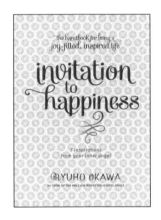

Hardcover • 176 pages • $16.99 • ISBN: 978-1-942125-01-3

There are so many beautiful reasons to be happy! This book is your invitation to a more joyful, authentic life. The pages inside offer practical tools for new habits for a more carefree, grounded, spiritual life. Through 7 inspirations, you'll be guided to the angel within you—the force that supports you to be courageous, inspired, and true to yourself. You'll find all the tools you need to live more confidently, peacefully, and authentically.

The Laws of Success
A Spiritual Guide to Turning Your Hopes Into Reality

Softcover • 208 pages • $15.95 • ISBN: 978-1-942125-15-0

The Laws of Success is the modern world's universal guide to happiness and success in all aspects of life. In these pages you will find timeless wisdom, the secrets of living with purpose, and practical steps you can take to bring joy and fulfilment to your work and to the lives of others. Ryuho Okawa offers key mindsets, attitudes, and principles that will empower you to make your hopes and dreams come true, inspire you to triumph over setbacks and despair, and help you live every day positively, constructively, and meaningfully. Your keys to a new future filled with hope, courage, and joy are just pages away!

The Heart of Work
10 Keys to Living Your Calling

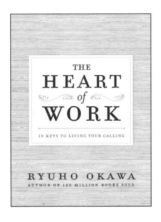

Softcover • 224 pages • $12.95 • ISBN: 978-1942125-03-7

Ryuho Okawa shares 10 key philosophies and goals to live by to guide us through our work lives and triumphantly live our calling. There are key principles that will help you get to the heart of work, manage your time well, prioritize your work, live with long health and vitality, achieve growth, and more. People of all walks of life from the businessperson, executive, artist, teacher, mother, to even students, and more will find the keys to achieving happiness and success in their special calling.

Think Big!

Be Positive and Be Brave to Achieve Your Dreams

Softcover • 160 pages • $12.95 • ISBN: 978-1-942125-04-4

This self-development book offers practical steps to consciously create a life of rewarding challenge, fulfillment, and achievement. Using his own life experiences and wisdom as the roadmap, Ryuho Okawa inspires us with practical steps for building courage, choosing a constructive perspective, finding a true calling, cultivating awareness, and harnessing our personal power to realize our dreams.

A LIFE OF TRIUMPH
Unleashing Your Light Upon the World

THE MIRACLE OF MEDITATION
*Opening Your Life to Peace, Joy,
and the Power Within*

THE ESSENCE OF BUDDHA
The Path to Enlightenment

THE LAWS OF JUSTICE
How We Can Solve World Conflicts and Bring Peace

MESSAGES FROM HEAVEN
*What Jesus, Buddha, Muhammad, and
Moses Would Say Today*

THE LAWS OF THE SUN
One Source, One Planet, One People

SECRETS OF
THE EVERLASTING TRUTHS
A New Paradigm for Living on Earth

THE NINE DIMENSIONS
Unveiling the Laws of Eternity

THE MOMENT OF TRUTH
Become a Living Angel Today

CHANGE YOUR LIFE,
CHANGE THE WORLD
A Spiritual Guide to Living Now

For a complete list of books, visit OkawaBooks.com.